by the editors of Sunset Books
and Sunset Magazine

ceramics

techniques & projects

Lane publishing co.· menlo park, california

foreword

The trend toward the making and collecting of handcrafted objects is greatly reflected in the growing popularity of ceramics. Classes in ceramics are proliferating across the country. The sale and exhibition of pottery is part of almost every craft fair, and ceramic ware is prominently displayed in galleries and gift shops.

Although many people believe that claywork involves a great deal of equipment and a spacious studio, much can be accomplished with only a few simple tools and a worktable. Designed for the beginning potter as a general introduction to working with clay, this book features discussions of basic techniques and suggestions for projects that can improve skills or be starting points for other ideas.

The preparation of this book was much simplified by the contributions of the many individuals who generously shared with us their experience and time. Particular thanks go to Viktoria Chulay, Gary Clarien, Ron Cooper, Veronica Dolan, Jack Feltman, Elizabeth Heil, Barry Horn, Judith Lange, Kay Lindquist, Peninsula Scientific, Eunice Prieto, Patricia Scarlett, Mr. and Mrs. Charles Sonett, and Toni Williamson.

supervising editor: Elizabeth Hogan
research and text: Jane Horn

Design: John Flack

Illustrations: Marsha Kline

Front cover: lidded casserole (page 58) and jug (page 73) designed by Elizabeth Heil; coiled trivet (page 30) designed by Jane Horn; photographed by Edward Bigelow.
Inside front and back cover: all photographs by Edward Bigelow except stoneware teapot photographed by Bill Haddox.
Back cover: triple hanging planter (page 27) designed by Jane Horn, photographed by Edward Bigelow.

Photographs: Most of the photographs in this book were taken by Edward Bigelow, with the following exceptions: Babcock and Wilcox Refractories Division, 9 left; Center of Asian Art and Culture, the Avery Brundage Collection, San Francisco, 4, 5 right; Charles H. MacNider Museum, Mason City, Iowa, 16; Ron Cooper, 47 top left; William Creitz, 58 top left, 67 left; M. H. deYoung Memorial Museum, San Francisco, 5 left, 66 left; Gregor Giesmann, 71 middle left; Bill Haddox, 59 bottom left; Diana Leon, 58 bottom left; Bob Nichols, 71 bottom left; Stanford University Museum of Art, 6 left, 78 bottom left; E. D. Taylor, 71 top right; Sharon Walker, 19; Darrow Watt, 79.

Editor, Sunset Books: David E. Clark

Seventh Printing April 1977

contents

ceramics...
an introduction

Simple, yet complex — ancient, yet so very contemporary — ceramics today is one of the most popular crafts among people whose interest in handmade objects and traditional art forms has been rekindled.

What advantages does ceramics offer the craftsman?
• The very impressionistic nature of clay permits the creation of an object that truly bears the mark of its maker, reflecting his touch, imagination, and skill. This potential for personal expression, combined with the natural quality of clay itself, makes claywork particularly attractive to a factory-based society.
• The evolution of ceramics has been so intimately related to the growth of civilization that it affords a comforting sense of communication with our past at a time when the present can be so rootless and changeable.
• Finally, ceramics is a craft that can be practiced at home without an expensive and space-consuming collection of equipment and materials.

LATE NEOLITHIC Chinese jar, dating from about 2,500 to 2,000 B.C., has a multi-color, painted spiral design on body.

The First Pottery

Clay had its origins in the beginnings of the earth. Its infancy as a useful material traces back to man's prehistory.

For thousands of years, clay lying in the ground bore the random impressions of the feet of nomadic wanderers roaming in search of food and shelter. With the evolution of a more settled, agricultural way of life, clay began to reflect man's domestication. Pottery fragments, showing a corded surface and dating back to prehistoric times, have led to the theory that early man first used mud to line baskets to make their containers more secure. As has been the case with many advances, it was probably by accident that man discovered that if these mud-lined baskets were placed in fire, they became hard and more durable. Eventually, the basket was discarded, and clay alone was fashioned into vessels for storage and into utensils for preparing and serving food.

The first pottery was hand built with coils, perhaps using a mold to shape the base. Primitive firing conditions left these pots black in color, quite porous and fragile, and basically devoid of all purposeful decoration except for some impressed patterns.

The appearance of the potter's wheel probably some 6,000 years ago in the Middle East and the development of more sophisticated methods of firing the ware gave ancient potters more control over their work. The wheel also turned what was basically women's work into a man's trade.

Early attempts at decoration consisted primarily of incising or impressing designs into moist clay and rubbing the pot with a smooth stone to develop a polished, more finely pored surface. Later, potters experimented with brushing on colored slips and coloring oxides. Examples have been found of Egyptian pottery some 5,000 years old embellished in these ways. The Greeks carried the art of slip decoration to high levels in the 6th and 5th centuries B.C.

Glazed pottery dating back almost 5,000 years has been recovered from Egyptian tombs. Other peoples didn't use glazes until much later.

The Contribution of the Chinese

One of the most significant advances in the evolution of ceramics (and one which greatly affected the course of the craft in most of the world) was the development of higher firing, stronger, and more vitreous clay bodies by the Chinese. Stoneware was being used by the Chinese several hundreds of years before Christ, and a porcelaneous stoneware appeared during the T'ang Dynasty (618-906 A.D.). A true white porcelain soon evolved and was highly prized by the Chinese and by many other cultures who attempted to emulate Chinese porcelain.

Over the next several hundred years, ceramics evolved both aesthetically and technologically — in kiln design, in the compounding of clay bodies, and in the formulation of glazes.

The older civilizations of the Middle and Far East had the greatest influence on the development of ceramics in the West, where its progress was slower. (It was not until the 18th century that the secret of making the much sought-after high-fire porcelain was discovered in Europe.) The advent of industrialization in the 18th century mechanized much of the production of European pottery, often at the expense of quality. Although folk pottery existed in Europe, the most sought-after ware in 18th and 19th century Europe was not native in design, but that based on Oriental or classical forms and motifs.

Settlers arriving in the Eastern part of the United States during the 17th century brought with them the pottery traditions of their native countries. Small local potteries produced plain, low-fire ware, and later, stoneware (after the trend in England towards high-firing bodies). However, up to and through the 19th century, imported pieces set the style for American potters.

The 20th century in Europe and America saw a reaction to the formal and classical in all areas of art and design, including ceramics. An attempt was made to simplify design and to work in harmony with the material being used.

GRECO-ROMAN *Attic black figure amphora, from about 510-500 B.C., has incised linear detail which was cut through black slip.*

CARVED CHRYSANTHEMUM *scroll pattern adorns body of 11th-12th century Chinese porcelaneous stoneware ewer.*

American Indian Pottery

On this continent, the earliest traces of pottery date back to about 3,200 B.C. in Ecuador and perhaps 2,000 B.C. in Mexico. Not until about 500 A.D., though, was pottery produced in any quantity in the American Southwest.

Pottery here developed along similar lines as elsewhere in the world. But the Indians of the Southwest never adopted the use of the wheel, nor did they ever develop a high-firing clay.

The earliest pre-Pueblo ware was molded in baskets and dried in the sun. Fired pottery was produced by about 400 A.D. A coil construction technique evolved that continues to the present day. In this method, the coils were smoothed over, then the piece was shaped and polished with a piece of gourd or smooth stone.

As Indian pottery developed among the peoples of the Southwest, surface treatment varied. Sometimes the coils were left partially or completely unsmoothed (called corrugated ware). The first applied decoration was simply black on white designs. These types of decoration appeared over several hundred years between 700 and 1050 A.D. Fine examples of black on white decoration were produced during the Great Pueblo period (1050-1300 A.D.). By the 16th century, polychrome (multicolored) patterns were being used with great success.

Today, Indian pottery is constructed in much the same way as in their prehistoric prototypes, and decoration is along traditional patterns developed hundreds of years ago.

Current Trends

Contemporary American pottery is a potpourri of styles and philosophies. The desire in this country for more personal, handcrafted ware has led to an increasing number of one-man potteries supplying their wares to the public through fairs, galleries, and shops.

At the same time, potters are also exploring the more abstract or sculptural possibilities of clay without attempting to transform it into utilitarian objects such as bowls, bottles, or cups. Although wheel-thrown forms are predominant, the flexibility and spontaneity of hand building is also attractive to today's potter.

Low-fire clay bodies and the bright, lustrous, low-fire glazes are making inroads on the popularity of the more traditional and muted stoneware. New methods of decoration (decals, silk screening, and photo-fabrication), in combination with a revival in the centuries-old luster-glaze technique, have transformed clay into a dynamic medium.

The expanding possibilities of ceramics as a vocation has resulted in an upswing in the number of ceramics classes offered. At no other time has the craft of ceramics been more accessible to more people.

As you begin to work with clay, you will be participating in a craft whose roots reach far back in time, yet which is today vibrant and flourishing. Ceramics is such a versatile craft that regardless of how you approach it — whether as a means of working off the tensions built up on the job or as a possible way of life — your experience will almost certainly be satisfying and rewarding.

SAN JUAN DRAINAGE water jar, from Great Pueblo period (1050-1300 A.D.), has corrugated finish (unsmoothed coils).

"HEART-LINE DEER" design on 19th century Zuni pot is distinctive to pottery of this Southwestern American Indian tribe.

THE CERAMIC PROCESS

A visit to a potter's studio — with its bags or tubs of fresh clay, shelves of yet unfired ware in various stages of completion, and groups of decorated and fired pieces — summarizes in a glance the attraction and excitement of claywork to both craftsman and collector.

No matter how experienced the potter, clay presents a continual challenge because of the endless ways it can be manipulated, its unpredictability, and the very personal nature of the final product. The metamorphosis of a lump of moist, plastic clay into a rocklike material after exposure to heat retains a magical quality despite the fact that the process has been explained scientifically.

Although technologically ceramics has become more sophisticated over the thousands of years since man first realized the potential of clay, the basic process has essentially remained the same.

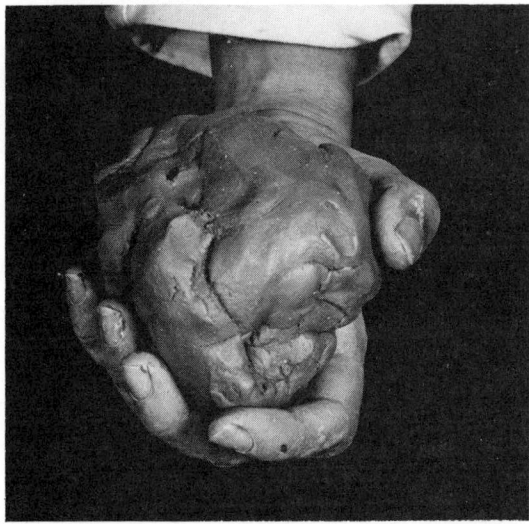

LUMP of moist, plastic, unformed clay is the common beginning for all ceramic ware, regardless of final form.

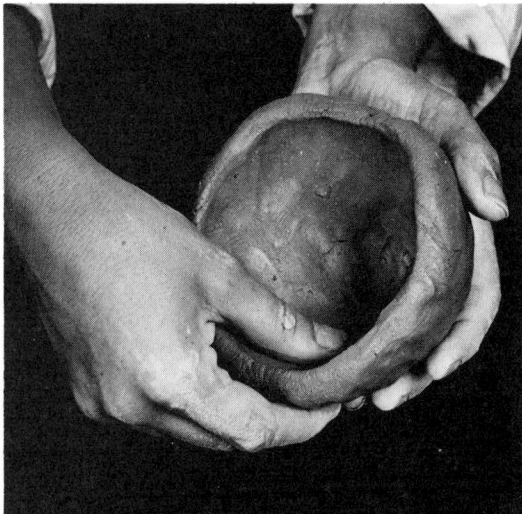

IN THE HANDS of a potter, unformed lump of clay is transformed into an object of planned design.

AFTER DRYING, clay object is bisque fired. Now it will not dissolve in water, is stronger than before.

FINAL STEP—bisqued piece is glazed (here in combination with oxides) and then subjected to a second, or glaze firing.

clay...
the basic material

When confronted with a lump of moist clay, most of us will pick it up and squeeze it between our fingers. The soft, pliant material, cool and pleasant to the touch, will probably invite further exploration. We might bend the clay, twist it, or mash it flat.

Plasticity

The ability of clay to deform under pressure and retain this new shape without cracking is called "plasticity." What gives clay this workability is its composition — made up as it is of microscopic particles shaped like elongated, thin, flat plates. These particles are so fine in size that the powerful electron microscope is needed to view them clearly.

When water is added to clay, it coats the particles so that they will slide across one another when handled, yet still be held together by molecular attraction. The finer the particle size, the more flat, water-lubricated plates there are and the more workable the clay. Therefore, clay with many of these tiny particles is more plastic than those clays more coarsely grained.

The best test of a clay's plasticity is simply working with it. Bending or twisting a clay rope or coil to see whether or not cracks develop is one test. A plastic clay will be able to withstand a greater degree of handling before fissuring than a less plastic clay.

While plasticity is a desirable and necessary property for any clay, very plastic clays have the disadvantage of high shrinkage. As clay dries, the water coating the particles evaporates and the particles pull together, causing shrinkage. Unless there is some way partially to hold back this movement, the amount of shrinkage could be detrimental to the finished piece. To reduce shrinkage, non-plastic "filler" materials (such as grog, flint, or vermiculite) are mixed into the clay body. A clay body is described as *open* when it contains an appreciable amount of these materials.

Grog is finely ground, already-fired clay. Because they have been previously dried and fired, grog particles won't change size as the clay body to which they were added

CLAY (shown here dry and cracked as it rests in the ground) is a natural material extracted from the earth's crust.

dries. As a result, non-plastic additives will reduce the movement of the particles of clay during drying.

Too much grog can make a clay too stiff to handle, so commercially prepared clay bodies usually won't contain more than 30 percent grog.

How Clay Dries

Clay begins to dry as the water film around each particle evaporates and the plates compact to fill the space left by the water. When the particles are in contact with one another, a piece is considered leather hard. By this stage, most of the shrinkage that will occur during drying has taken place. However, water is still present in the clay.

Although the ideal situation would be to have all the clay particles line up, this doesn't happen. Spaces, or pores, which trap water (called pore water) are left between the irregularly arranged plates. The particles themselves are also still moist. Pore water evaporates slowly, for access to the clay surface has been blocked by the touching particles. The clay is ready for firing when it is bone-dry or no longer cold to the touch. The final completion of drying can only be achieved in the kiln (see firing, pages 74-77).

Ware that has been dried but not yet fired is called raw, or *greenware*.

Potters who attempt to dry out their pieces on a hot, sticky day will quickly learn that the amount of humidity in the air and its temperature will affect the drying rate. An atmosphere with a high moisture content will retard drying. Drying is speeded up by heat and by exposing a piece to a stream of forced air.

Problems in drying. To prevent warping and cracking of drying ware, the drying must be even and slow. Uneven drying, especially of flat surfaces, such as slab tiles and boxes, encourages warping; the particles of areas that dry more quickly will pull together first and lock into place before slower drying surfaces have had a chance to shrink. Allow air to reach all sides of a piece equally. Dry ware

on a rack so air can reach the bottom.

It may be necessary to cover a freshly made object with plastic to retard its drying. Thinner sections and small appendages, such as handles or feet, are usually protected with plastic to slow down and equalize their drying rate with the rest of the piece. If possible, dry tiles between two plaster bats, layers of newspaper, or on an open rack; turn them gently but frequently.

Types of Clay

Clay is the result of the decomposition or erosion of the earth's rocky crust into minute particles of varying size. Granite-type feldspathic rock is the source of all clays.

Basically, clay is composed of alumina, silica, and chemically combined water. Its molecular composition is $Al_2O_3 \cdot 2SiO_2 \cdot 2H_2O$ in its purest state, but, in reality, clay

CLAY SHRINKS as it dries. The bottom, dried bar was originally the same size as the moist, freshly cut bar above it.

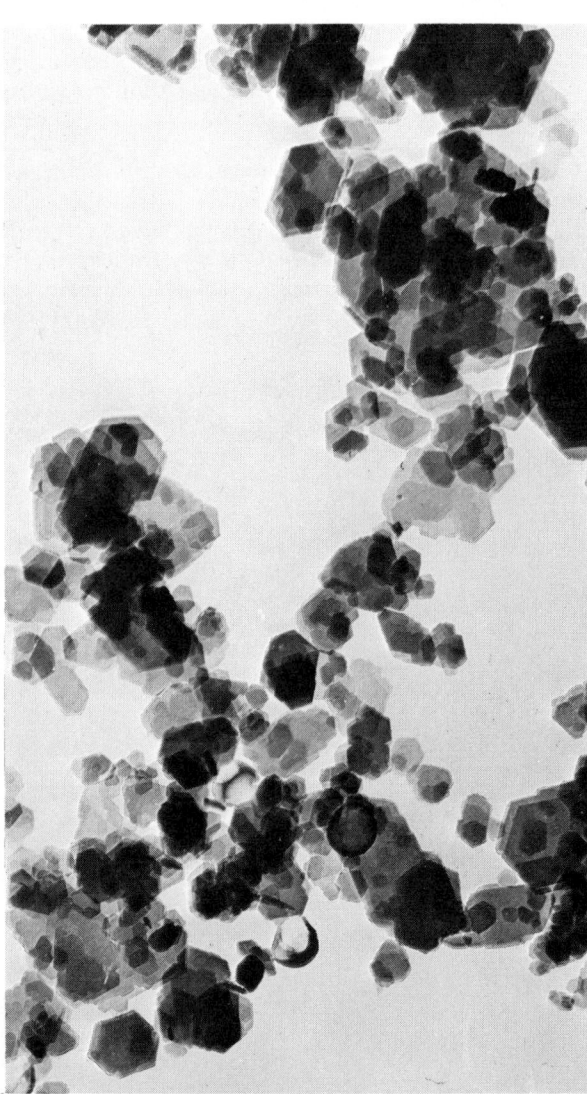

ELECTRON MICROSCOPE picture of kaolin (a type of clay) particles, magnified 40,000 times, shows flat, plate-like shape.

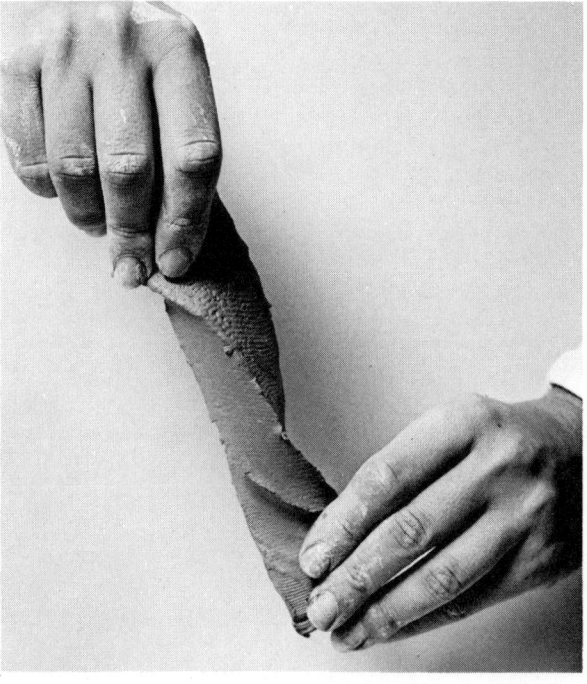

TWISTING CLAY is one way to test for plasticity. Plastic clay holds up longer when worked than less plastic clay.

also contains iron and other impurities that affect a clay's color and lower its melting point.

Although there are many sub-classifications, clays fall into one of two broad categories: residual or primary clays and sedimentary or secondary clays. Those clays which stay close to the site where they were formed (the "parent rock") are called *residual or primary clays*. Relatively unaffected by the elements, they have a coarse particle size and are not very plastic. They are more or less free of impurities, retaining a whiteness of color and a high resistance to heat. Primary clays are usually blended with other materials to make them more workable. High-firing porcelain clay bodies include primary clays in their composition.

Other clays are moved from their origins, usually by water, but also by wind or even glacial action. When they finally come to rest, these *sedimentary or secondary clays* are finely grained because of the grinding action of moving rivers and streams on the clay particles and because heavier particles have already settled out at earlier stages of the journey. Therefore, they are more plastic than primary clays. Sedimentary clays have undergone a change on their journey, mixing with other materials as they are transported. The clays that you will use are, as a rule, of the sedimentary type.

Kaolin, a very pure, natural clay and white in color, is never used by itself because of its relative lack of plasticity and its resistance to heat except at very high temperatures. Kaolins are important ingredients in the formulation of whiteware bodies.

Ball clays are relatively pure (although not as much as kaolin), high firing (to about 2400°F.) natural clays which fire close to white in color. They are fine-grained and plastic but aren't used alone because of their high shrinkage rates. Ball clays are often added to clay bodies that contain kaolin to render them more plastic and workable.

Fireclays can be either plastic or coarse and unworkable. Their characteristics vary except that all fireclays are extremely refractory or high firing (to about 2700° F.) and are used to make firebrick, to line kilns and fireplaces, and for kiln shelves and posts. The presence of some iron in fireclays imparts a cream to tan color to the fired clay.

Stoneware clays, very popular with potters, vary in their plasticity and in drying and firing characteristics. They can be used alone if these characteristics combine into a workable material. More often, stoneware is a blend of natural clays, plus other ingredients added to obtain a desired degree of plasticity, color, and maturing temperature. These clays are high firing, maturing between about 2200 and 2300° F., and range from light tans to darker browns and greys when fired. Because they become hard and vitrified when fired, they do not need to be glazed to hold water.

Earthenware is either a single natural clay or a mixture of several clays that fires to a relatively low temperature (1700 to 2100° F.) because of impurities (fluxes) that lower its melting point. The fired body is only partially vitrified and therefore remains porous, is subject to chipping, and

COMMERCIALLY PREPARED clay is available wet in 25-pound bags, dry in 50-pound units. Dry clay powder is less expensive to buy and easier to store, but it must be mixed first with water, then kneaded to evenly distribute moisture.

will not hold water without being glazed. Fired earthenware ranges in color from white to buff and light tans, pinks, reds, and browns.

Porcelain is a compounded clay composed of white burning clays, kaolin, and ball clay, along with fluxes and silica. Porcelain is a very high-firing clay (between 2500 and 2700° F.). When fired it becomes white, translucent, very hard, and vitreous. Its low plasticity makes porcelain difficult to work with.

What Clay to Use?

By experimenting you will get to know the characteristics and uses of various clays and which clays work best for different types of projects.

Although many potters find digging for and preparing their own clay very exciting and satisfying, beginning potters are advised to work with commercially prepared clay bodies. Purchased clays are categorized by type (for example, earthenware, stoneware, and porcelain), the temperature range to which they should be fired, and recommended use. Some clays are specifically designed for throwing on the potter's wheel, whereas others have been compounded for sculpture or hand building.

Clay can be bought wet (in 25-pound bags) or dry (in 50-pound bags). Dry clay powder is less expensive than moist clays but requires extra work on the part of the potter. It must be mixed with water (and possibly other ingredients) and worked on to homogenize moisture content.

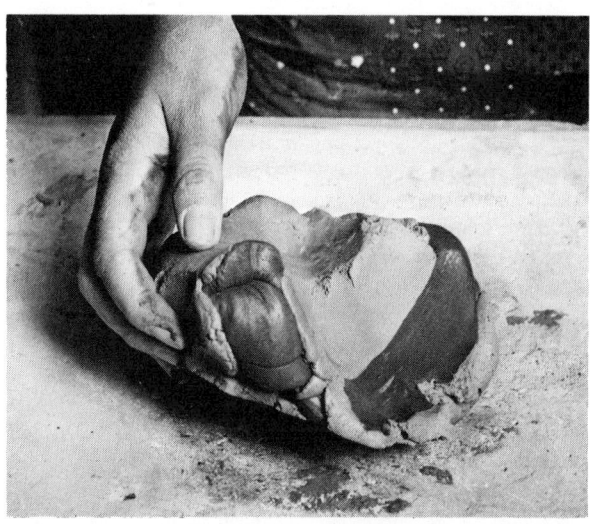

1) THIS SEQUENCE of pictures, using two colors of clay, demonstrates how clay is homogenized through wedging.

2) TWO CLAY COLORS have been slapped together and, through the wedging process (see next page), are beginning to blend.

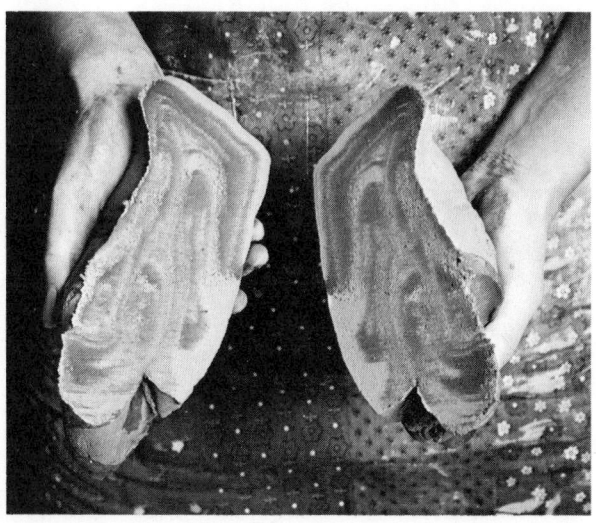

3) CONTINUED wedging blends the clays even more. Slice through the clay at this point to see marbled pattern.

4) WITH WEDGING almost completed, only faint lines of the lighter color clay can be distinguished on the surface.

Dry clay is easier to store than large bags or tubs of wet clay, for it takes up much less room in the studio or workshop — an important consideration for the potter with a limited work area.

Wet clay can be stored in heavy plastic bags or large plastic trash cans with a tightly fitting lid. Care should be taken that the clay doesn't dry out in storage from prolonged exposure to air. Plastic cans can also be used to mix up large batches of clay made from clay powder and water, and perhaps other ingredients. The blended clay is mixed and stored in the same container, saving you work in transferring the material to another storage tub.

Preparation of Clay

Before you can start to shape an object out of clay, the clay must be of the proper consistency: not too moist or too dry, uniform, and free of air pockets that may interfere with throwing or cause a piece to crack or explode in the kiln.

A fresh, unopened bag of commercially prepared clay can be used without any further conditioning if a check has been made for air holes, which, if present, must be worked out.

Sometimes, though, new clay or clay scraps that have sat unused for a period of time are too stiff or dry to work with. You can increase the moisture content of any clay by slicing it into thin sheets and sprinkling the slices with water. Clay that is too moist and sticky can be dried on a plaster surface that will absorb the moisture.

Clay that has stiffened in its container and which is not needed for immediate use can be made moist several ways. Punch holes in the clay and sprinkle it with water, or wrap the clay in wet cloths and close off the bag or can, letting it sit for a while. This aging process, aside from increasing the moisture content of the clay, seems to make it more workable.

Wedging

After the clay is sufficiently moist, it must be wedged or kneaded to distribute the moisture content evenly, homogenize and remove lumps and irregularities, and force out any trapped air.

Clay can be wedged or kneaded several ways. Many potters combine methods or develop their own techniques, but it doesn't really matter how you prepare your clay as long as it accomplishes the desired result.

Special wedging tables or boards with plaster or cement surfaces are most often used for wedging clay. Usually a length of wire is strung diagonally from a support set on the table and attached to the front of the frame.

Where space is a factor, small, portable wedging boards can be made of cement or plaster enclosed in a wooden frame.

If you work in an area of your home where no room is available for even a small wedging table or board, clay can

be prepared on a wooden table top or any surface to which the clay won't stick.

One method for wedging is to slice a squared-off lump of clay into two or more pieces. These pieces are thrown onto the table one on top of the other. This is repeated until the clay is smooth and free of holes (see page 13).

Often a spiral wedging procedure is used in conjunction with the first method or by itself. With practice, you can prepare relatively large amounts of clay in this way. A jelly roll effect is created by pulling the clay up from the back of the mass, pushing back down into the mass, and then lifting it up and forward. This rocking and twisting motion forms a "tail" that is continually worked into the clay. Spiralling the clay mass into itself and then out ensures a more uniform consistency (see page 13).

When using this method, be careful not to push the clay back and down so hard that folds develop which will form air pockets. To prevent the clay from spreading out too thinly as you knead, compact the ends occasionally as you are working.

To save time in future work sessions, wedge scraps of clay into a usable mass before storing.

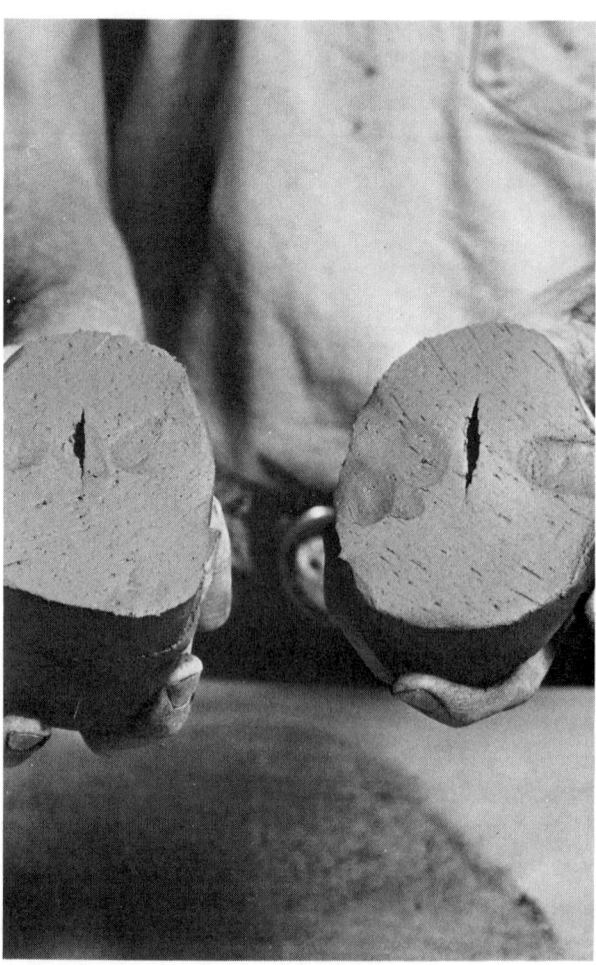

WEDGING removes pockets of air trapped in clay. Air holes may cause a piece to distort while being worked or crack when fired.

Slicing Method

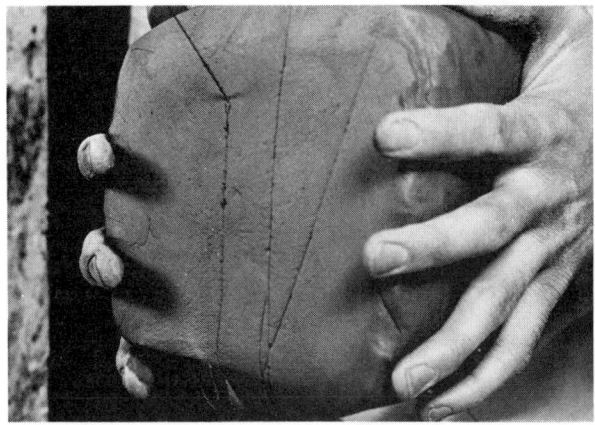

1) SLICING CLAY, here with a wire strung across a wedging table, exposes much of the clay surface, revealing irregularities.

2) SLICES OF CLAY are slammed one atop the other to smooth the clay and to force out trapped air.

Spiral Method

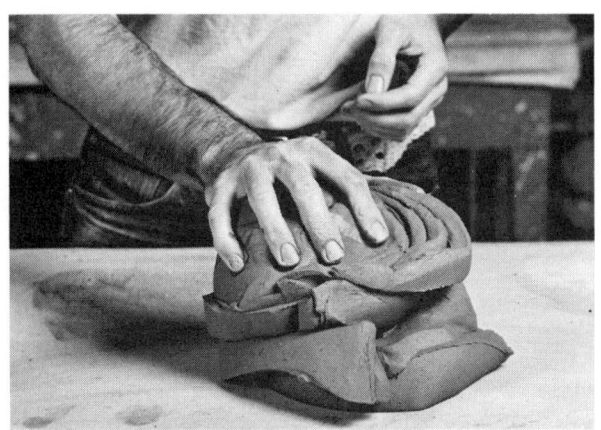

1) SCRAPS OF CLAY are being pressed together for wedging. Wedging is essential—it creates a uniform mass of clay.

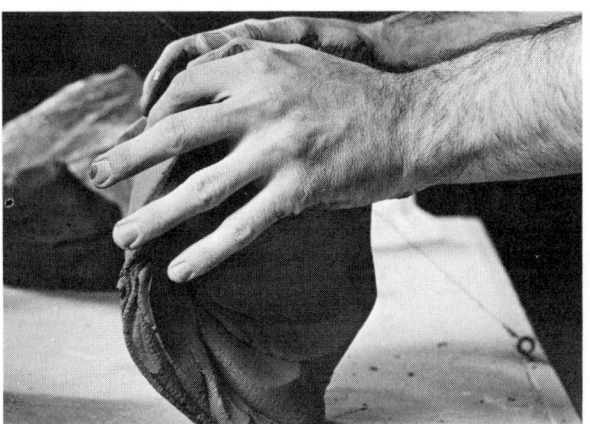

2) FOR SPIRAL WEDGING the clay is first lifted up from the back and brought forward, forming a "jelly-roll" effect.

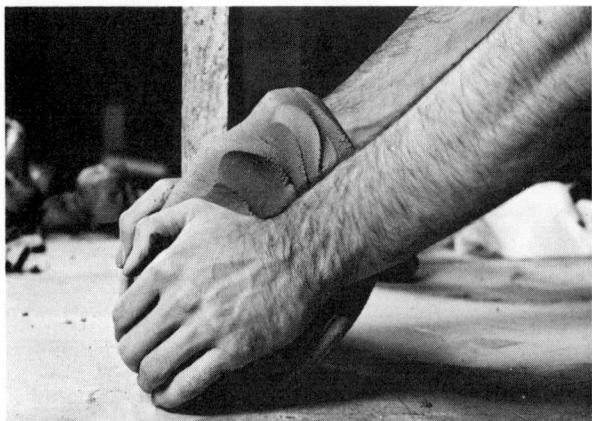

3) CLAY MASS is then pushed away and down into itself with a rocking and twisting motion that spirals the clay.

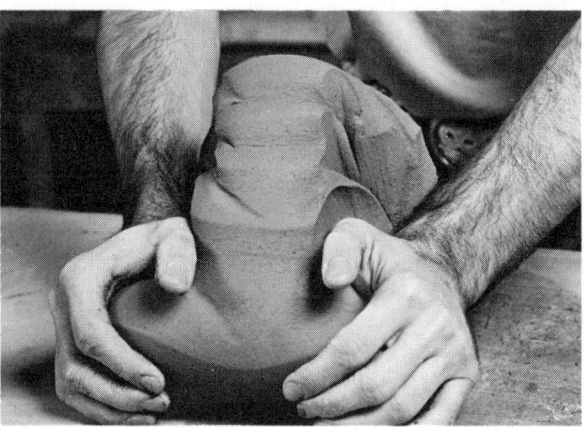

4) PROJECTING "tail" or "spine" of the wedged mass shows the ridges that develop as the clay is wedged by this method.

tools
for the potter

The very flexible "do your own thing" nature of ceramics is best illustrated when you consider the tools used by potters in forming, decorating, and shaping clay objects. Although many tools are specially designed for claywork, many less expensive substitutes are available if you seek them out and adapt them to your needs or make them yourself. The rule of thumb should be to use whatever does the job best for you.

Standard Equipment

After you've had experience in working with a variety of tools, you may find that you favor some and hardly ever use others. The equipment discussed below represents a starter set of implements that you might use from the start to the finish of a piece.

Rolling pins or dowels are used to prepare clay slabs of even thickness. You can texture slabs by first wrapping the rolling pin with a coarse weave cloth. Rolling pins make good molds for slab work.

Calipers help promote uniformity when throwing, particularly in matching lids to pots.

Brushes are used for applying decoration. Pointed Japanese brushes allow great freedom of design, while flat brushes give an all-over coating of slip or glaze. Wax for dry footing or for wax resist can be applied with either type of brush.

Sgraffito tool, with a wooden handle and pointed metal ends, is used for making linear patterns in clay or for cutting through slip or glaze for the sgraffito technique.

Fettling knife is a special potter's knife, although many potters commonly use ordinary household paring knives for trimming, carving, and slicing clay.

Needle or pin tool, a thin needle projecting from one end of a wooden or metal handle, has a myriad of uses, including trimming, scoring, and decorating.

Wire cutter is commonly a length of wire or strong nylon cord attached to wooden dowels. This device is used to

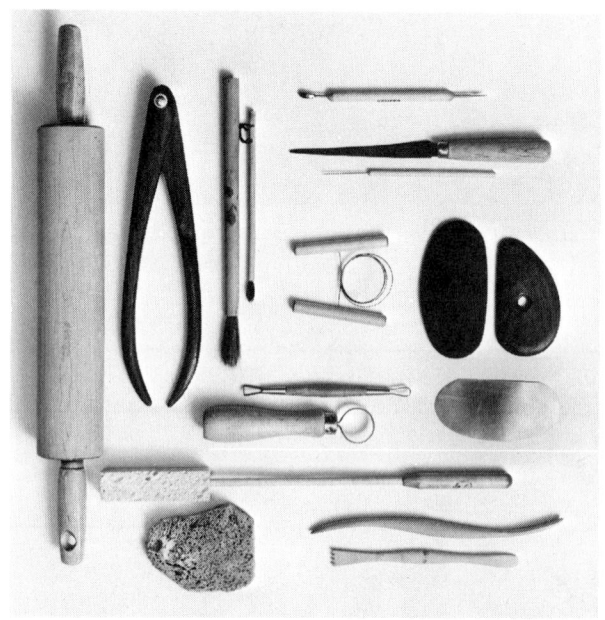

COLLECTION of tools pictured here and described below under Standard Equipment are commonly used by most potters.

cut pieces off the wheel head or bat. You can make a wire cutter with piano wire or nylon cord and two empty spools of thread or two clothespins.

Ribs (also called kidneys) are made of curved hardwood or rubber and are used for shaping pieces on the wheel.

Wire, loop, and ribbon tools are made of wood with a loop of thin wire or flat metal at either end. Trimming, carving, and decorating are just a few of their many uses.

Scraper is a flat, flexible metal tool used for smoothing clay surfaces, texturing, removing excess clay and slip, and developing true angles.

Sponges for ceramics are usually of natural origin and come in a variety of sizes. They can be used to moisten clay for throwing, wetting edges in preparation for joining, smoothing, and removing excess water. A long-handled sponge gives access to the interior of narrow-necked or deep pieces.

Modeling tools are among the most useful. Basically, these hardwood tools are used on a shaped but still plastic clay form to move clay across joints and seams, to create texture, to smooth surfaces, and to reach otherwise inaccessible interior spaces.

Other equipment you will find helpful:

Bats are used as portable work surfaces. Usually round and approximately ¾ to 1½ inches thick, they can be made of plaster (which will absorb excess moisture from clay), wood, or plastic-topped composition board. Bats are often set on the wheel head for a throwing surface, allowing freshly thrown pieces to be removed easily for drying and freeing the wheel for another project.

Banding wheels are round turntables (metal, plastic, or a composition material) that allow the potter to see all sides of his piece. These wheels are often used for coil building and for brushing or spraying on slips and glazes.

Wedging table or board can be simply a wooden board. However, a table or board topped with cement or plaster and which has a wire for cutting clay makes the best surface.

Paddles, flat wooden sticks (often textured), are used to alter the original shape of a clay form or to add texture.

Pot lifters, made of metal, are used to remove freshly thrown pots from the wheel.

Chuck is usually a bisqued clay cylinder, pinched in at the middle and open at the top and bottom. Chucks are used for trimming narrow-necked pieces which can't be propped directly on the wheel. The pot is set into the chuck which is attached to the wheel head with lumps of clay.

Ruler is useful for measuring slabs and, if made of wood, for paddling.

Miscellaneous Equipment

Much of the equipment a potter might use was not originally intended for ceramics but fulfills particular needs.

Plastic bags are perfect for storing clay. Plastic over unfinished pots keeps them in a workable condition by helping to slow down drying and allowing pieces to dry more evenly. Plastic also serves as a lining for molds.

Large plastic trash cans with lids make excellent storage bins for clay. Plastic buckets can hold water, slip, or glaze; plastic containers and jars can store slip, glazes, and glaze ingredients.

Wooden sticks of varying thicknesses and lengths serve as guides for rolling out or cutting slabs, as drying racks, or as a rack for glaze pouring when set over a container. Wire cake racks or discarded oven or refrigerator shelves can also be used for drying pots or pouring glaze.

Sheets of wood, composition board, or masonite make good portable work surfaces. Cover with canvas or oil cloth (shiny side down) to keep clay from sticking to the board as you work. Use other kinds of cloth (either fine or coarsely woven) to cover worktables for rolling out slabs, to cover unfinished work, or to line molds.

Atomizers can be used for spraying water onto pots that are drying too fast. Plastic squeeze bottles or a rubber ear syringe are suitable for applying and trailing slip.

Kitchen pads (made of non-woven, webbed material) or wire mesh screening smooth rough surfaces. Have glue, either epoxy or silicone adhesive, also on hand for repairing broken parts or attaching pieces.

Plaster

Plaster has many uses in the potter's studio: making bats (a pie tin coated with a separator, such as mineral oil or butter to release the hardened plaster, makes a good mold for bats, as does a plastic utility bucket which doesn't need a separator), molds, stamps, and as a surface for wedging.

Special casting or pottery plaster available from ceramic suppliers is typed mainly by use and setting time (usually anywhere from 20 to 30 minutes). When mixing up a batch of plaster, follow the manufacturer's or dealer's recommendations as to proper plaster-water proportions. As plaster remains in a workable state for a limited time, have all your plaster projects in mind before you begin mixing.

To mix, slowly sprinkle the plaster over water until the plaster is no longer absorbed. Stir the mixture with your hands or a whisk to remove lumps, being careful not to incorporate any air. Use immediately.

Let any leftover plaster harden in its container, then chip the hardened mass into pieces and discard. Never throw unwanted plaster down the sink.

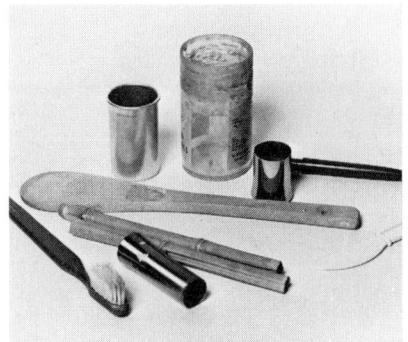 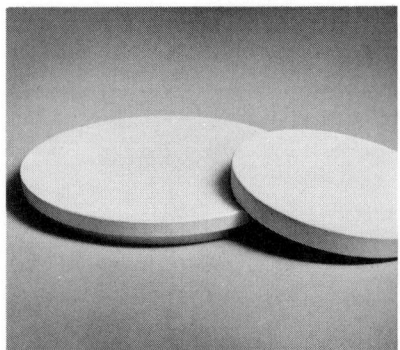 

HOUSEHOLD OBJECTS (left) can be better suited for certain procedures than specially designed tools. Buy plaster bats (center) or make them yourself. Bisqued cylinder (right), called a chuck, holds narrow-necked pots for trimming.

techniques
for hand building

In the midst of creating an object from clay, few potters will stop to think, "I am now pinching a pot," "coiling a bottle," or "building a box with slabs." However, what you want to make often determines what technique you choose. Or conversely, what technique you wish to work in can determine the nature of your final project.

This chapter has been divided into the four basic hand-building techniques: pinch, coil, slab, and molds. A brief discussion of several terms common to the four methods is given below. At the end of the technique section is a portfolio of ideas for finishing your pot. Since non-wheel techniques represent an easier, more spontaneous, and less expensive introduction to the craft, throwing on the potter's wheel is described separately (see pages 48-59).

After acquainting yourself with the basic techniques, you can apply what you've learned by working on your own specially designed project or ones described in the Ideas for Hand Building chapter (see pages 26-47).

Terms for Basic Techniques

In the basic technique discussion and in the project instructions, several terms appear frequently that should be defined before you begin work.

Scoring. To join two pieces of clay, it is usually necessary to prepare the surfaces of each piece to create a strong bond where they meet. Generally this is done by making regular incisions with a pointed or serrated tool, a needle, or a fork across the joining areas.

Slip. Liquid clay, the consistency of mayonnaise, is used to coat the scored surfaces of two pieces of clay that are to be joined. Slip functions as a glue.

Modeling. To make joints more secure and to smooth over seams, clay is modeled or drawn across the seam with a wooden modeling tool or your finger.

Smoothing. A smooth object, such as a stone, the bowl of a spoon, or the flat end of a modeling tool, can be used to refine the surface of a partially completed pot. A damp

DESIGN: DENNIS JENNINGS

TWO TECHNIQUES, pinch and slab, were used to form this hand-built, lidded stoneware jar.

sponge will also level lumpy areas and soften unwanted sharp edges. Sponging brings out grog by drawing away the clay, making grog particles more prominent.

Scraping. A thin, flat metal tool called a scraper is helpful in developing an even surface, removing excess clay or slip, and sharpening corners. Scraping groggy clay will emphasize grog particles and create an attractive rough texture.

Paddling. Beating clay with a flat stick is referred to as "paddling." Paddling strengthens joints, thins walls, develops the contours of your pot, and can even reshape it. Paddling is also a means of creating surface texture.

pinch method

DESIGN: JANE HORN

PINCHING A POT is often the beginning project. This glazed earthenware bowl was decorated with a stamped design.

The pinch method is the easiest introduction to working with clay. It usually requires a minimum of clay and no equipment other than your hands. Because only your hands are manipulating the clay, pinching is an excellent way to develop a sensitivity to clay and to gain an understanding of the material's plastic nature.

Pinched pottery dates back thousands of years. Today, lovely pinched tea bowls from the Orient are admired for their simplicity of form and their pleasing asymmetry.

The bowl is the most common pinched shape. After you have mastered the pinch "pot," you can advance to goblets, cups, spoons, pitchers, planters, containers, and dishes — all of which use the bowl as part of their construction.

Pinched pots do not have to stand alone. They can be joined rim to rim to make spherical or ovoid forms (see page 29) or side by side into clusters (see page 28). Because of their simplicity, pinched pots lend themselves to all manner of texturing and glazing. The pinch method can be used in combination with other hand techniques, producing exciting and sophisticated pieces.

Whatever you decide to make by pinching, remember that you are working with your hands. Don't try to reproduce the mechanical perfection of thrown forms; enjoy the irregular surface and spontaneity of hand-built ware.

When making pinched forms, use a clay of medium plasticity. This type of clay will help to keep the walls of your piece from sagging and, at the same time, keep them from becoming so stiff they crack.

Forming the Basic Pinch Bowl

Begin with a wedged ball of clay (about the size of a baseball) that you can comfortably hold in your hand. Smooth it by rolling in your hands; shape it by slapping with your hands. Holding the clay ball in one hand, insert the thumb of the other hand into the ball, leaving a base thickness of about $1/4$ to $3/4$ inch (this thickness depends on the final size of the pot and how you plan to finish the bottom). Open the pot by pinching (or squeezing) the clay lightly between the thumb and fingers, at the same time slowly turning the clay with the same hand until you come to the starting point.

It's very important to develop sensitivity to wall thickness by touch. (A good way to do this is to close your eyes and go over where you've just pinched.) When you're satisfied that the walls are uniform all around, move your fingers up from the base and pinch again, turning the pot as you work. Don't march your fingers up and down the pot to shape, but spiral them from bottom to top. This will help maintain evenness. As your form grows, it becomes difficult to get your fingers back down to the base to correct the wall thickness.

Remember that pinching leaves finger marks. You can leave the finger indentations on the outside for decoration or smooth them out as you rotate the pot.

Clay shapes dry from the top first, so keep your rims slightly thicker than the lower wall to combat cracking. To slow down the drying, dampen your hands slightly as you go, particularly along the slope between thumb and forefinger which rubs the rim as you pinch. Or spray a light mist of water on the pot. If the edges do crack, apply water with a damp sponge and gently work in the moisture to heal the cracks. Use water sparingly, for too much water can cause the pot to collapse.

When your bowl is finished, stabilize its base by tapping gently on a flat surface, then let it stiffen on its rim to prevent the shape from sagging. When your pot can be handled without distorting or is leather hard, add texture. At this stage, also add feet, handles, or other attachments (see page 25). For a polished surface, rub the pot with a smooth stone or with the bowl portion of a spoon.

Continued on next page

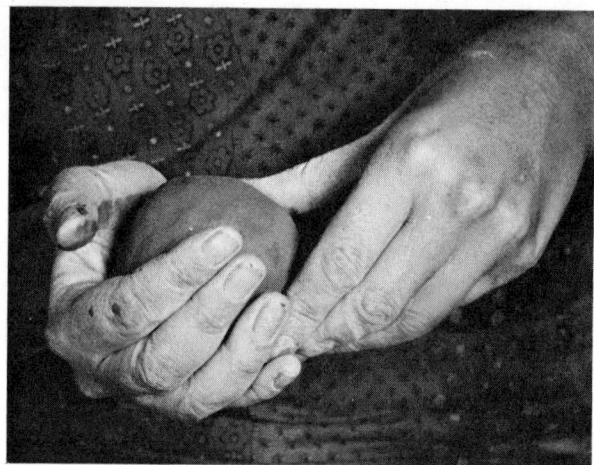

1) BEGIN PINCHING a bowl by inserting your thumb into and almost to the bottom of a smooth ball of clay.

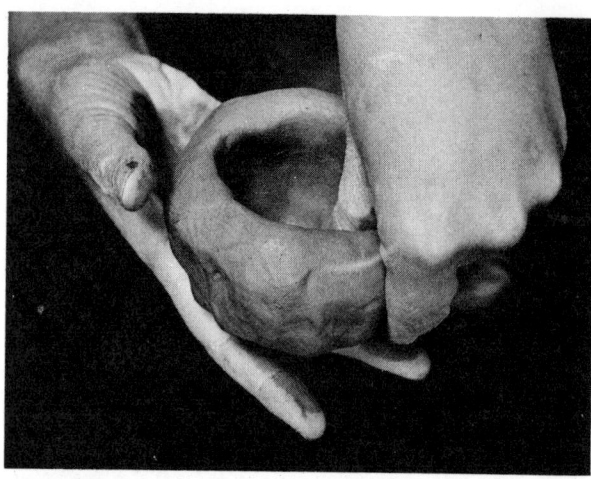

2) ENLARGE THE THUMBHOLE by squeezing the clay between thumb and fingers while slowly rotating the pot.

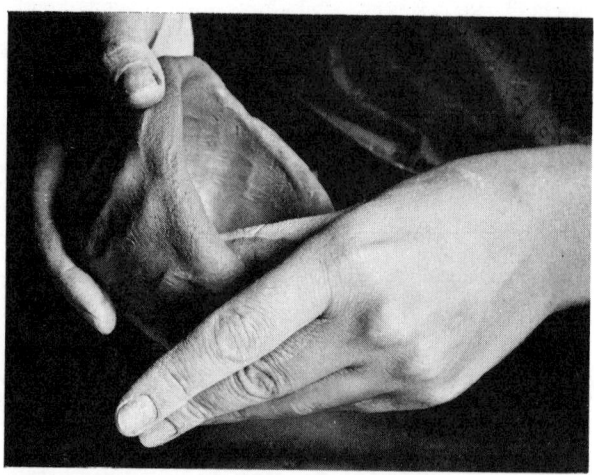

3) THIN THE WALLS by continuing to squeeze clay between your fingers with even pressure. Note finger marks.

4) DEVELOP THE FORM by drawing clay from thicker to thinner areas with a wiping motion of your fingers.

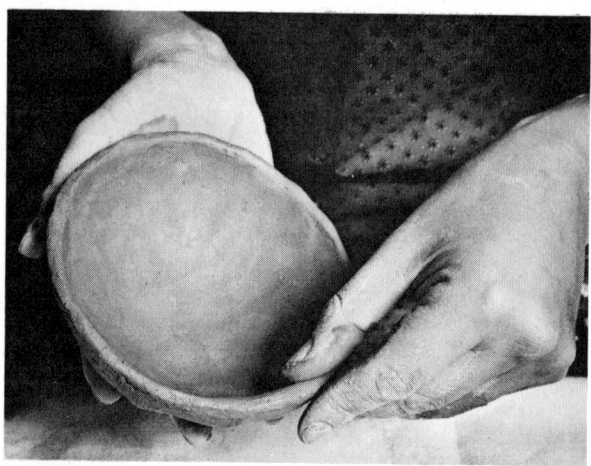

5) FINISHED POT should have uniformly thick walls. Let it stiffen somewhat before handling further.

6) RUBBING INSIDE of a leather-hard pot with a stone will develop a smooth, polished surface.

coil method

DESIGN: BRUNO LAVERDIERE

COILS can be built up into large, dramatic forms. "Disc Monument" with oxide decoration is 36 inches high.

Before the development of the potter's wheel, coil building was the traditional method for making pots. In parts of Africa and among Indians living in the American southwest, coiling is still the basic technique. Though coiled pieces may appear primitive in comparison to thrown forms, pots of great refinement were and still are being made.

Coiling is not as difficult as it may first appear. With practice you can learn to produce coils uniform in length and width and of the proper consistency. Coiling does take time, but potters using this method like the peaceful rhythm of developing a coiled form, the control they have as they work, and the pleasure of progressing at a leisurely, measured pace.

Of all methods of hand building, coiling has the most potential hazards. If you consider a coiled piece as a stack of seams with clay in between, the importance of securing the seams to avoid cracking becomes apparent. As each horizontally worked coil dries, it shrinks and pulls away from those above and below. Unless you've joined each row well, you could end up with a number of clay rings instead of a pot.

If the coils have been joined well on the inside, you can leave the outside coils as they are for a ribbed effect. But it is safer to strengthen the bonds between the outer surface coils by either partially or totally smoothing them over or by impressing a pattern over the seams.

Whether you work your coils horizontally or take advantage of the unique flexibility of this method by rolling the coils into convoluted "building blocks," the crucial test of the success of your pot is how well it holds together during the drying and firing. A coiled piece should be dried very slowly, the first day or so under plastic. Large forms may need several weeks to dry. So that air can reach all surfaces, place your drying pot on a rack of some sort — perhaps several sticks arranged a few inches apart.

When coiling a large pot, stop when the piece is partially completed. Let it stiffen slightly so that when the remaining coils are added, the lower walls won't sag out of shape. If you interrupt your work for any reason, protect the top coil with a damp cloth. If you stop coiling for an extended period, cover the piece with plastic. Before beginning again, score the top coil, moisten it with water or slip to restore plasticity, and then proceed. If you skip this step, the newer clay will contract more than the already constructed body, and the stress will lead to fissuring.

Use a grogged clay slightly stiffer than normal to keep the coils from stretching as they are lifted. Roll coils on a damp surface. Either stretch a cloth over a board or use 3/8-inch plywood; moisten the surface with a sponge as you work. Scoring and slip aren't necessary for joining coils if the clay is kept plastic.

Coil building is easier if you work on a turning device. Although a metal banding wheel is perfect, it is expensive. More reasonably priced plastic turntables are available from a ceramic supply house, in the housewares section of a department store, or in a hardware store. Place newspaper, a board, a plaster bat, or a paper-covered serving tray over the turntable so that your piece can be removed easily.

When rolling coils, give yourself as much room as possible, for your coils can only be as long as your worktable. Because of space limitations, 30 inches will be probably the longest your coils will grow, but that is sufficient for large shapes. It is better to make coils longer than you need. Frequent patching can be annoying and does add extra weak spots.

The diameter of the coil depends on the final size of your pot. Smaller pots call for thinner coils, larger pots for thicker coils. Coils ½ inch in diameter will allow flexibility in pot size and prevent overly thin walls.

Making Coils

Squeeze a wedged lump of clay until it resembles a thick rope. Try to keep the "rope" even by rotating the clay as you squeeze to minimize finger marks. The smoother the rope, the easier it is to roll out a coil. (Oriental potters pull coils from a rope held vertically, without rolling.)

From about a 7-inch piece of rope, roll out a coil. Place dampened hands, fingers flat, in the center of the coil; move your hands out as you roll the coil in a complete 360-degree revolution. Avoid rocking the coil just back and forth, for this will cause it to flatten. When rolling, maintain an even pressure to avoid creating thin spots or breaks. If your clay sticks, the work surface is too damp; if it cracks, either the clay or the work surface is not damp enough.

Make many coils at one time (about 10 or 12) to avoid unnecessary interruptions. More coils can be rolled as your piece stiffens. Cover coils with a damp cloth until you are ready to use them.

Building with Coils

Make a base by flattening a wedged lump of clay with your hand; even the clay with a rolling pin. From this slab, cut out the base. The thickness and diameter of the base depends on the size your pot will be and how much trimming you will do.

Lift one coil, being careful not to stretch it, and, with one hand, lay the coil on the base. With the thumb of your other hand, use a wiping motion and join the coil to the base on the inside (the fingers of this hand support the outside). When joining coils, always pull the clay from the side of the coil, never from the top, down over the clay below. Turn the piece as you go until one revolution has been made. Bevel the ends where they meet and join securely. Work in the coil on the outside in the same manner as on the inside, turning the piece in the opposite direction. Add subsequent coils the same way. Some potters prefer to cut off a coil after each rotation; others continue spiraling until the coil is used up.

After coiling several rows (but no more than about five), support the outside wall with your hand and scrape the inside smooth. If you want a smooth outside surface, scrape it also.

To expand your form, lay a coil on the outer edge of the coil below. To contract your form, place your coil towards the inside edge.

When your pot is finished, trim away excess clay at the base. Refine the piece further with a smooth stone or damp sponge. Paddle to thin the walls or change the shape of the pot. Add feet, a spout, or handles when the pot has stiffened somewhat (see page 25).

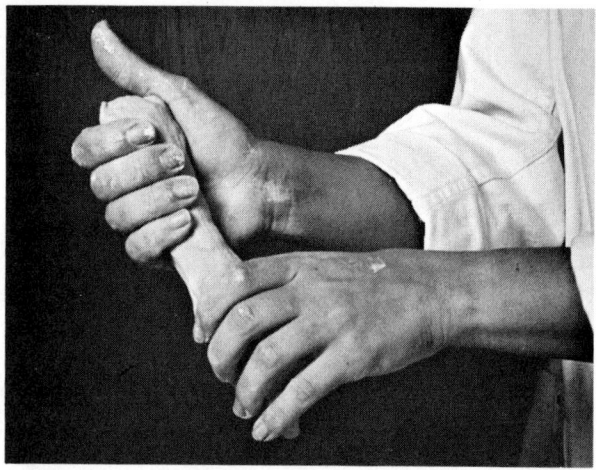

1) START A COIL by squeezing a lump of clay into a smooth, even, thick rope, about 7 inches long.

4) MAKE A BASE for a coiled pot by cutting out a disc with a pattern from a flattened clay slab.

7) SMOOTH THE INSIDE SURFACE by scraping. Support the outside of the wall with your hand as you scrape.

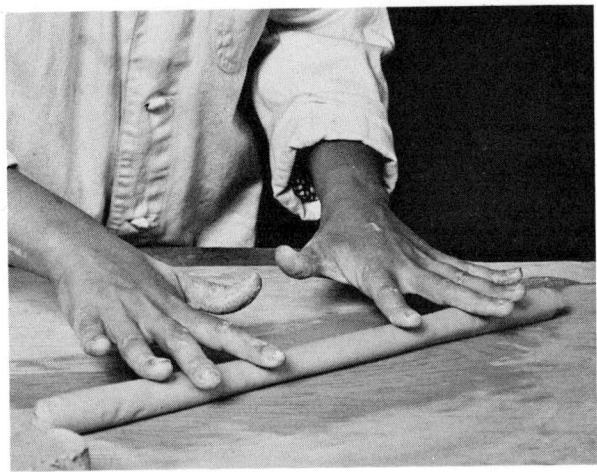

2) TO MAKE A COIL, place hands in the center of the coil; move them out towards the ends as you roll the clay.

3) ROLL MANY COILS at one time. Cover unused coils with a damp cloth to keep them moist until needed.

5) FASTEN FIRST COIL onto base by pulling clay with your thumb from the side of the coil down onto the base.

6) TO EXPAND COILED FORM, lay the coil so that it rests on the outer edge of the coil below.

8) TO CONTRACT A COILED FORM, lay the coil towards the inner edge of the coil below.

9) PADDLE YOUR COILED PIECE to change its shape, thin its walls, or add texture.

slab method

DESIGN: FLORENCE MOORE COHEN

BY THEIR NATURE, slab forms are well-suited for decoration. Note luster and glaze pattern on stoneware box.

Although ceramic tiles are perhaps the most familiar slab-made objects, the simple slab can be manipulated or combined to form a wide variety of shapes: boxes, cylinders, plates, mobiles, jewelry, planters, containers, and sculptural forms. Regardless of what you decide to make, a thorough understanding of this technique will help you turn out well-built slab pieces.

Slabs should be made from wedged, open and grogged clay. Wedging homogenizes the clay, removing lumps; grog reduces shrinkage, helping to counter warping. Grog also makes clay less plastic and stronger for self support.

Four Ways to Prepare a Slab

Slabs can be prepared several ways: pressing, rolling, throwing, and slicing. Rolling is perhaps the simplest, but it is more a means of crushing the clay into shape than a technique which takes advantage of the composition of the material (see pages 8-13). Still, rolling does develop a slab of even thickness.

You can texture your slabs at the same time you make them by covering your working surface with a coarse fabric. Use an open weave cloth (burlap, canvas, or the underside of oil cloth) to prevent the clay from sticking.

Pressing a slab. Flatten a lump of clay by patting it with your hand. Thin the flattened mass by pushing out from the center with the heel of your hand. Make sure to work from center to edge to evenly compress the clay.

Rolling a slab. Decide the width of your slab and place a guide stick on either side of the partially flattened clay. The distance between the sticks will set the slab width, and the thickness of the guides will regulate the thickness of the slab. Generally, a good workable thickness is $\frac{1}{4}$ to $\frac{1}{2}$ inch. Wooden guide sticks in these thicknesses are available from lumber yards and home improvement centers.

Rest a rolling pin or dowel on the sticks at their center point and push along the guides always from the center out until the clay is uniform. Make sure your roller is wider than the slab and clean of scraps. If both sides of the slab need to be free of crease marks that may occur from a less than taut cloth, flip the clay and roll again. This will, however, blur any texture.

Throwing a slab. This is an excellent way to produce slabs of even thickness without any equipment. Prepare a thick, flat, uneven clay brick about 1 to 2 inches thick, as you did when pressing a slab. Lift the clay at the far end and flip it down onto the worktable towards you so that it slides as it comes into contact with the table top. The top edge of the clay should hit first; the rest will spread and thin as it meets the table. After several throws, the slab will be uniformly thick, although slightly thinner at the edges. With a little practice, the technique will come quite easily.

Slicing a slab. Another quick way of producing multiple slabs of equal thickness is cutting sheets of clay from a well-wedged clay block. On both of the long sides of the block, stack the same number of $\frac{1}{4}$ or $\frac{1}{2}$-inch-thick sticks. With a wire cutter or strong thread, pull through the clay along the guides. Remove a layer of sticks for each slab.

Pre-stiffening the Slabs

After you have prepared your slabs, let them stiffen anywhere from half an hour to overnight, depending on how stiff you need them for your piece and the amount of moisture in the air. If the slabs are to be left overnight, cover them loosely with plastic. Pre-stiffening is particularly important when making boxes or other straight-sided pieces as it allows the clay to undergo some shrinkage, causing the finished pot to contract less when drying. It also means that the walls will have the strength to stand firm. Be careful not to overdry the clay; otherwise it may crack when cut and lack the plasticity to join well. Slabs for curved and molded forms will crack when shaped if they are too stiff, so it's best to let them stiffen after shaping.

Building with Slabs

After you decide on a project, cut out the components. Use paper patterns or templates for straight edges, matching walls, and true angles. (Paddling and scraping the constructed piece also develops angles and straightens sides.)

To join individual units, score edges to be joined and wet with water or slip (sometimes both). If your clay is well-wedged and quite pliable, it's possible to join slabs without slip. This is risky unless you are sure of your material. For more strength, work a thin coil into each joint and paddle the seams with a flat stick. When working on rectangular pieces, rest the largest part on the bottom for maximum support.

Joints are potential trouble spots. As the clay shrinks, strains may open what you thought was a secure seam. To avoid this, try to minimize the number of seams by folding a slab instead of joining. And see that the components of your piece are fastened together securely.

Allow an even flow of air around your piece as it dries.

Set a tall piece on a rack (wire mesh or several sticks), covering it with plastic to equalize the drying rates of the upper and lower sections. Newspaper stuffed into container shapes helps absorb moisture from the interior and encourages even more the drying of the pot. You may have to wait to use the rack until the base is dry enough not to be distorted by the rack.

Note: tiles require careful drying. If you're using a fine-grained clay, cut several shallow grooves on the backside to allow air to penetrate the clay, for tiles tend to curl if dried unevenly. Sandwich tiles between two flat plaster bats, layers of newspaper, or plastic to dry. When a tile is leather hard, elevate it on a rack until completely dry, turning often for uniform exposure.

When slab pieces have stiffened somewhat or are leather hard, apply texture to them. Slabs can be textured before they are cut into shape as long as the design won't be distorted by handling. Decoration works particularly well on slabs because of their flat surface.

1) PRESS A SLAB by pushing clay out with the heel of your hand from the center of a flattened clay lump.

2) ROLL A SLAB with a rolling pin or dowel. Use two guide sticks to ensure even thickness.

3) FLIPPING A FLAT BRICK of clay onto a table is a fast but more difficult way to make slabs.

4) MULTIPLE SLABS can be made by slicing through a block of clay. Guide sticks make for uniformity.

working with molds

Using molds enables you to make more than "one-of-a-kind." Basically, molds for claywork fall into two categories: those into which clay is pressed and those over or around which clay is shaped. A third method, slip casting, uses a mold in combination with liquid clay.

The press mold. This type of mold can be fashioned of many materials, ranging from a specially made plaster brick or bowl hollowed to receive the clay to nontraditional molds such as a kitchen bowl, earthenware planter, baking tin, pie plate, cardboard container, or a sling of cloth supported on a frame. Carved styrofoam and cork make good press molds because they add both texture and pattern.

In a press mold, clay lines the inside walls or fills the entire mold cavity (tiles, for example). The interior walls of the press mold can have an incised or relief pattern which will be picked up by the surface of the clay that rests against the mold.

Carved patterns can be freeform or geometric. Remember the pattern in the mold is the negative of the finished clay piece. Carved designs should be free of undercuts that might trap the clay.

Unless the mold is of porous material (such as plaster), it must be lined with a cloth, damp paper strips, or plastic to allow the clay to dry without sticking.

The press-mold method is good for making dishes. Prepare a slab of uniform thickness, one that is larger than your finished piece will be. Line the mold with clay; gently smooth the clay with a damp sponge to conform the clay to the mold. Trim the edges with a needle or knife. When the dish is stiff enough to handle, separate it from the mold. By this time the clay will have shrunk away from the mold and can be removed easily. The dish can be smoothed further by scraping or with a damp sponge when it becomes leather hard.

Drape molds. A drape mold can be cast by pouring plaster (see plaster, page 15) over a clay shape, removing the clay when the plaster has set, and pouring more plaster into this "waste mold" (which has been coated with a separator such as oil or a soap solution). When the plaster has set, it is removed and the mold is ready. A plaster drape mold can also be created by pouring plaster into a bowl or cylinder (also brushed with a separator), letting it set, then removing it. Other drape mold possibilities are a dried clay form covered with cloth to prevent sticking and a variety of "found" objects (smooth rocks, tin cans, a rolling pin, cardboard tubing, or containers). Wrap non-porous molds with waxed paper, cloth, newspaper strips, paper toweling, or discarded nylon hosiery to prevent sticking.

(See page 43 for step-by-step instructions for making a plate over a drape mold.)

When using a drape mold, keep in mind that the clay must be removed as soon as it is stiff. Clay shrinks as it dries; if left on the mold too long, particularly over plaster which is very absorbent, it will crack.

Don't attempt to drape a form that curves inward at the rim, for it will be impossible to remove later on.

Clay can be molded completely around a form if there is some way to remove the mold. Balloons punctured before the clay is leather hard or a wad of newspaper that will burn away during the bisque firing are two suggestions for easily removing a mold. You can make a box by covering a rock or other similarly shaped object with clay, then slicing the clay into two pieces to remove the mold (this forms a lid and a bottom). A wad of clay tucked into each corner of the lid will act as flanges to hold the lid in place.

Slipcasting. This technique allows a potter to make duplicates quickly. To slipcast, pour slip into a hollow one or two-piece plaster mold. The action of the plaster as it draws moisture from the clay forms the walls. Wall thickness depends on how long the slip is in contact with the plaster. When the walls are as thick as you want, pour off the excess slip. As the piece dries, it shrinks from the plaster and can then be removed.

Solid slip casting — plates for example — takes place in a mold whose cavity is the shape of the finished piece.

Special casting slips and molds are available from ceramic suppliers.

MOLDS needn't be specially designed. Look around house and garden for suitable, unusual, interesting shapes.

necks, lids, spouts, handles, feet

One of the pleasures of working with clay is that you can produce objects that are both decorative and functional. A simple cylinder can be transformed into a handsome mug by adding a handle. Give it a spout and you've made a pitcher. Two handles and a lid create a casserole. Any addition — lid, neck, spout, handle, or foot — should relate to and be in harmony with the basic shape of the pot. Equally important, attachments (with the obvious exception of a lid) should be fastened securely to the body.

It is usually necessary to cover small attachments with plastic when they are added to a partially dried piece to equalize the drying rates.

Necks. Form a neck by pinching in at the shoulder of your pot, by paddling, or, if your piece is constructed with coils, by gradually reducing the length of the coils and then stacking them until you have the height you want. Or, hollow a narrow cylinder or thin rectangle of clay by wrapping clay around a dowel. If a neck is to be added to a closed form, be sure to open the pot where it meets the neck to avoid explosions in the kiln.

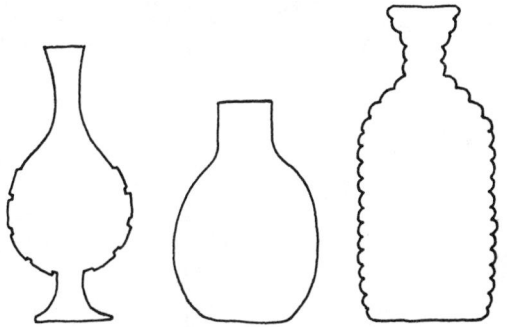

Spouts. Pull a spout while the clay is still plastic. Draw the rim of your pot forward with the index finger of one hand and between the thumb and forefinger of the other hand which are resting lightly against the rim about 1 to 2 inches apart. Use the index finger to pull the spout through. A spout can also be cut from a slab and added, but you must remember to cut open the wall behind the spout for pouring. Shape a coiled spout by laying on longer coils so that the wall projects outward at one point.

Lids. No matter how you make your lid, it's necessary to ensure that it rests firmly on its base (see page 57). If the lid fits in a pot, it needs to sit on a projection of some sort. A coil or narrow strip of clay added to the inside rim of the pot will serve this purpose. A lid that is flush with the lower walls should have a flange. Again, a coil or clay strip projecting down from the lid or up from the pot works well. The flange for a teapot lid should be quite deep so that the lid stays on the pot when tipped for pouring. If you're working with a closed form, cut off the lid in a jagged fashion or at an angle.

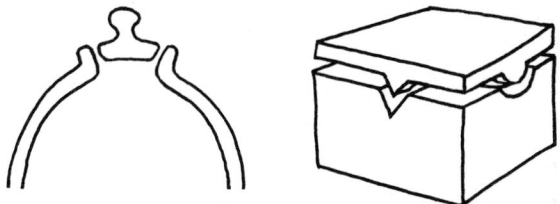

Handles. Handles can be cut from a slab or fashioned from coils. They can also be pulled from a lump of clay (see page 57). Attach handles when the pot is leather hard to avoid distortion. To fasten, score both pot and handle, "glue" with slip, and seal the seams. Adding clay around the joins of both handles and spouts provides extra strength.

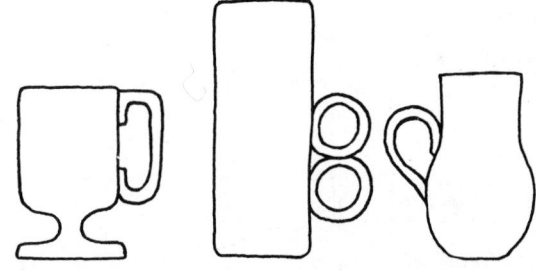

Foot. A foot can be made easily by hand. Attach a coil or narrow slab strip to the underside of a leather-hard pot for a base or use several balls or cubes of clay. For some reason, three feet will always sit level whereas four may wobble. If enough clay has been left at the bottom of the pot, a foot can be developed by trimming on the wheel (see page 56).

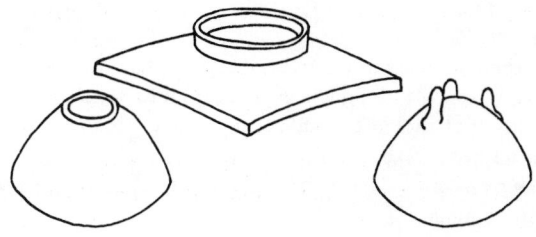

ideas
for hand building

SLAB wall hanging, see page 39.

Since the possibilities for developing moist and pliant clay into a purposeful form are almost endless, let your first encounters with clay be detached experiments in shape and texture. Gradually develop a feel for the material; don't be pressured into making something right away. It's probably best, although admittedly very hard, to discard your efforts of the first week or two.

When you are ready for a more structured experience, you may wish to begin with the ideas offered on the next 18 pages.

The projects in this section can be easily made with a few basic tools in a limited work space. Each is intended to provide experience in working with clay, allowing you to explore the properties of the different materials used to create pottery. After this initial introduction to the medium, you should be comfortable enough with the various techniques to proceed on your own.

All the projects in this chapter are hand built, rather than thrown on the wheel, to demonstrate what can be achieved without the outlay of time and money demanded by wheelwork. However, many of the designs can be adapted for the wheel.

Keep in mind that the projects are merely suggestions — goals to work towards as you learn. Clay offers so many opportunities for variety that experimentation should be your uppermost goal. Make all of your pieces a personal statement.

When you begin a project, it's not always necessary to have a specific design in mind. Clay has a spontaneous quality that should be realized in your work. But a shape can be overworked, so if you are not sure of the next step, back away and study what has been accomplished so far. Then continue.

Note that many variables need to be considered within each project, such as the type of clay used, form, and decoration. Remember that the pieces illustrated are just one way to approach the idea. Look to nature for both shape and decorating inspiration. Most museums have a pottery collection. Study past solutions to universal design problems to stimulate your imagination.

It would be most unusual if you already had a kiln in your home. Schools, ceramic supply stores, and local potters often will fire your pieces for a fee computed on the size of what is to be fired. Track down a kiln source first so you can buy materials geared to the temperature at which that particular kiln will be fired.

Tools needn't be specially purchased. Forks, spoons, empty pill containers, popsicle sticks, and pebbles are just a few of the creative (and money saving) substitutes found around house and yard.

A final note: before beginning a project, carefully read the instructions. Helpful hints are given to prevent possible problems. It's a good idea to review the technical discussions in the individual chapters on clay, technique, decoration, and firing.

triple hanging planter

See also back cover.

DESIGN: JANE HORN

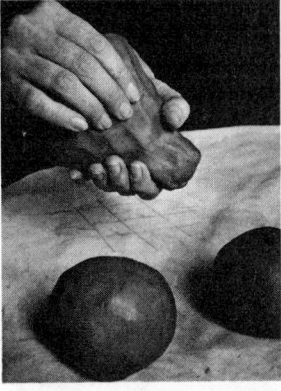

FOR EACH POT leave about 1-inch-thick base to shape into drain (top left). Open drainage hole after planter is formed (top right). When somewhat dry, apply texture (bottom).

Pinched forms can be both utilitarian and sculptural. The end result is mostly limited by the amount of clay you can comfortably manipulate in your hand. This triple-pot hanging planter is one suggestion as to what can be accomplished with simple shapes. Many variations are possible, so experiment with form and with surface decoration.

The bisqued pots were brushed with a thin coat of Barnard clay slip, which turns dark brown-black after firing, and then wiped with a damp sponge so that any depressions retained the color of the slip and the raised areas stayed clean. For a particular effect, repeated spongings may be necessary.

Use a baseball-sized ball of clay for each pot. Pinch open the clay ball, leaving a base thickness of about 1 inch for the drain. Thin out the walls to approximately 1/4 inch but keep the rim thick. Fold over the rim and invert the pot on a flat surface to level rim. Pat the rim's underside to flatten further. Pinch in just above the rim to shape the body. Pull out the thick base to finish the drain.

With your thumb, smooth the inside of the pot to even the walls and push excess clay down to the drain or up towards the rim to elongate and enlarge the basic form. Continue to shape and smooth until you have the shape you want.

With a modeling tool, flatten and smooth the rim further; trim with a needle. Make three evenly spaced holes in the rim for hanging. Cut off the top of the drain extension and, using a straw, punch out the drainage hole. Smooth the drainage hole perimeter and flare the drain at the bottom.

When the pot is dry enough to handle without distorting or is leather hard, smooth with a scraper, a sponge, the flat end of a modeling tool, or a smooth stone. Apply decoration at either of these stages.

Use strong leather or cord to hang the fired pots. Knot the cord under each of the hanging holes to hold the planter in place. Measure the cord before knotting so the planter will hang evenly.

a cluster of pots

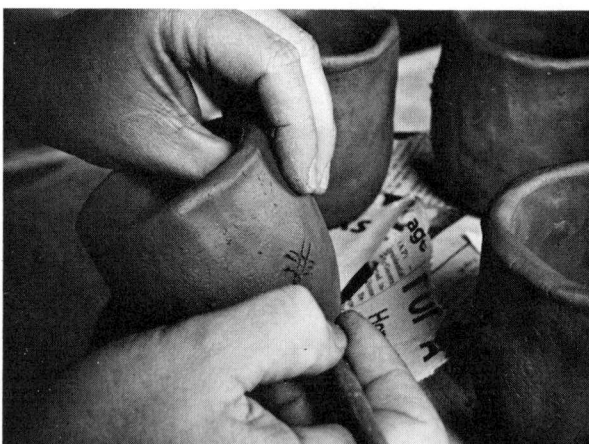

Combining several pots in clusters expands the possibilities of working in the pinch method. Clustered pots can either touch directly or be joined through the use of clay "extenders," as we have done here. This particular grouping is intended as starter pots for herbs. Although these pots are in a ring, they can be joined side-by-side.

Labels identifying each herb are simply clay discs attached to heavy wire. Stamps to letter the labels are made from alphabet noodles (available in most food stores), individually glued to thin sticks or dowels (used fireplace matches are good). Make sure the dowel is smaller in diameter than the letters, or the impression will be distorted.

To start, pinch five pots of approximately the same size. Next, form five clay plugs for the joins, flaring the ends for easier attaching. Arrange the pots on individual pieces of newspaper so that as the cluster dries, the shrinking clay form can contract without stressing the joints.

Score each pot where the clay plugs will be attached. Also score both ends of the plugs. Cover the scoring with slip and, with your thumb supporting the inside of the pot to prevent distortion, firmly press plugs to pot. After all the parts have been joined, finish shaping by pushing out at the inside bottom of each pot with your fingers. Smooth both inside and outside surfaces with a modeling tool, a scraper, a sponge, or a smooth stone. Form rims when the pots have dried somewhat; cut out a drainage hole in the bottom of each.

To make the labels, flatten and smooth a small ball of clay. Punch a hole in the top center for the wire stems.

Both pots and labels were stained at the bisque stage with black-burning Barnard clay slip, wiped with a damp sponge, and then re-fired.

SCORE POT (top) and plug where they will meet; apply slip over scoring. Firmly press plug to pot, supporting pot with your thumb (middle). To letter labels, stamp clay discs with uncooked alphabet noodles glued to wooden sticks (bottom).

banks from joined pots

DESIGN: JANE HORN   DESIGN: TONI WILLIAMSON

a needle before paddling to release trapped air that could press at the inside seam and cause cracking.

When the pot is leather hard, cut out the top opening and the slots with a thin, sharp hobby knife. Smooth the inside seam with a tool.

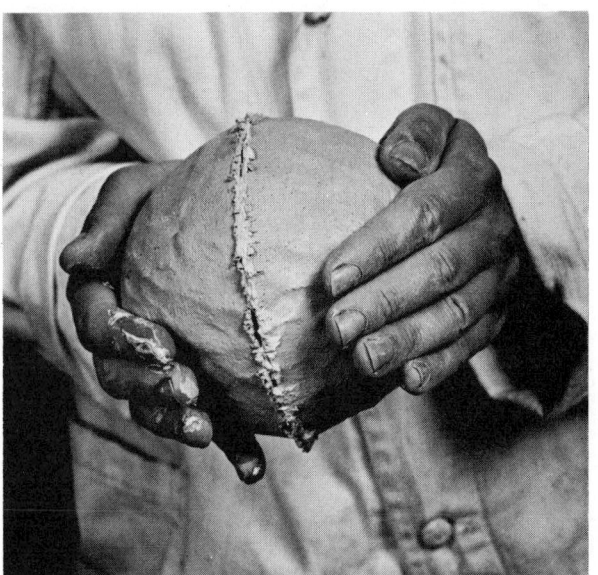

Closed, spherical, or ovoid forms are created by combining two pinched bowls having the same diameter and wall thickness. With a little practice, you should be able to control your pinched forms enough to produce the duplicates needed for combining.

The possibilities for expanding on this technique are many. Necks, handles, feet, spouts, and all manner of embellishment can alter the combined form. The project described here is a bank made from two pinched bowls, with coin slots incorporated into the design. The traditional bottom opening has been moved to the top and closed with a cork. After the pots were bisque fired, several contrasting-colored glazes were poured over the round pot and brushed in rings on the taller pot.

As shown, the form can be either rounded or elongated. Decide on the final shape, then pinch two bowls that will join to achieve the form you want. (Keep the first bowl covered while you are pinching the second.) Level the rims for an easier join and finish the inside of each pot with a modeling tool, a scraper, or a smooth stone. Invert the bowls on a flat surface and wait until they have stiffened sufficiently enough to be handled without distorting before proceeding.

To join, score the rims and coat with slip. Press the pots firmly together. With a wooden tool, pull clay over the joint from above and below it, scoring as you work. Roll a coil of clay about 3/8-inch thick and press it into the joint; then smooth it.

With a flat stick, paddle the pot to smooth and shape. It may be necessary to pierce the piece at the top with

JOIN TWO slightly stiffened pinched bowls of the same size and diameter (top). For accuracy, outline top hole and coin slots, then cut each out with sharp, thin-bladed knife when pot is leather hard (bottom). With a long tool, smooth interior of pot.

two styles of trivets

See also front cover.

DESIGN: JANE HORN

Woven and curled trivets are good beginning coiling projects — they call for practice in making and working with coils, yet both can be quickly completed. Other projects that lend themselves to coiling practice and fast completion are flat wall plaques and weed holders.

Woven trivet. The coils are combined in a basket weave pattern. Although this trivet is square, a rectangular shape is also possible.

From cigar-shaped wads of clay, roll out several long coils about ½ to ⅝ inch in diameter. From these, cut eight coils, each about 8 inches long, for weaving. Make each of the eight somewhat longer than the desired trivet length and width, for the coils "shrink" when woven.

Arrange four coils in parallel rows. Place the remaining four perpendicularly across the first four. Score the clay where the coils will touch. Remove the top layer of coils; coat the scoring with slip. With one of the upper coils, begin weaving into the bottom row, alternating over and under. Repeat with the remaining coils.

With your finger or anything that will make an impression, press down where coils cross. This will push the slip into the scored coils to seal. Trim the ends of the coils.

Curled trivet. Although these coils were curled into "snails" of similar sizes, coils lend themselves to any number of fanciful patterns. Whatever your design, remember to smear the coil patterns smooth on one side to prevent cracking. Unless the clay is very fresh and plastic, it will probably be necessary to score and add slip as you work.

Roll seven coils into snail-like designs. Decide which side will be the bottom, then smooth over the coil seams completely. Score and coat with slip where the pieces will join. With your finger or a modeling tool, pull clay across the joint to secure and continue pressing along the seams with a tool to compress the joints more firmly.

  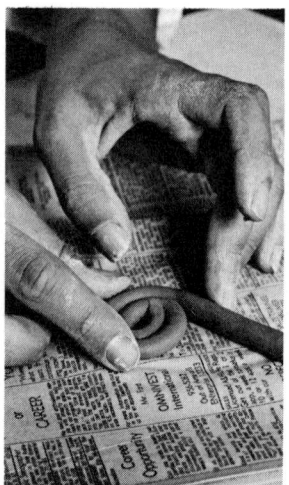 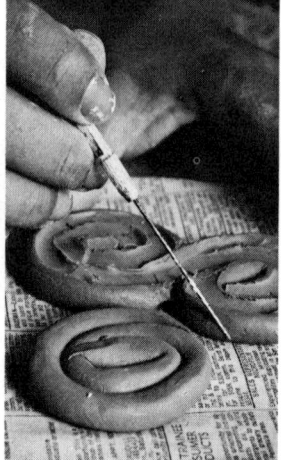

WOVEN TRIVET: score, cover with slip where coils will touch (left). After weaving, press down to secure joins (right).

CURLED TRIVET: roll coils into "snails" (left). Press "snails" together; indent along seams with a modeling tool (right).

large coiled bottle

Although the novice may have difficulty working with the large mass of clay needed to throw oversized shapes, coil building allows you to make large-scale pieces quite easily. This demonstration shows coiling a tall bottle, but the final shape can be whatever you choose. The important lesson of this project is that with coiling, the beginner can develop forms otherwise beyond his technical ability. Experienced potters often find a sense of freedom and flexibility when working with coils that is not possible with other methods.

If you work fast, the bottle can be built at one sitting. There is a danger that the walls of a big piece can slump from the weight of the clay, so it may be necessary to let the lower section stiffen slightly under plastic. If you choose this approach, be sure to score the top coil and apply slip before continuing; otherwise the piece may crack.

Because of its size, the finished bottle may need to dry slowly, perhaps for as long as a week or two. Therefore, build your piece on a portable working surface. Loosely cover the piece with plastic for the first several days of drying, allowing some air to reach the bottle.

To begin, pat out a thick base, about 1 inch. If your clay is very moist, scoring and slip won't be necessary. Start laying on coils, remembering to smooth joints between coil layers by pulling clay down from upper to lower coils. Continue building, smoothing over the inside and outside surfaces, until you have the shape you want. To expand your form, place a coil towards the outside edge of the coil below. To bring in, lay the coil towards the inner edge.

As you progress, step back from time to time and analyze your piece for form. The shape can be altered by pushing with your hand or paddling with a flat stick.

Although the inside was worked smooth with a scraper, finger marks were left on the outside for some decoration. To finish, stain or pour a glaze over the pot after it is bisque fired.

 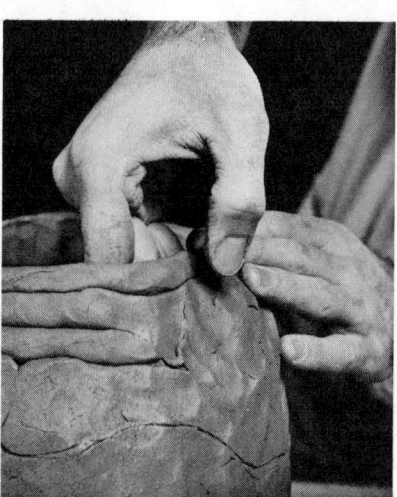 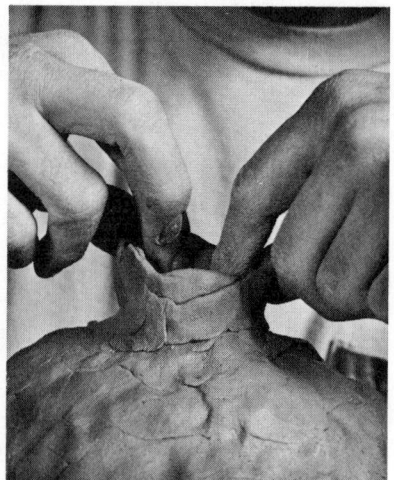

COILED FORM was contracted by laying coils towards inner edge of coil below (left). Coils were smoothed together; finger marks (center) were left as decorative element. To form neck (right), add on very small coils.

coiled cylinder

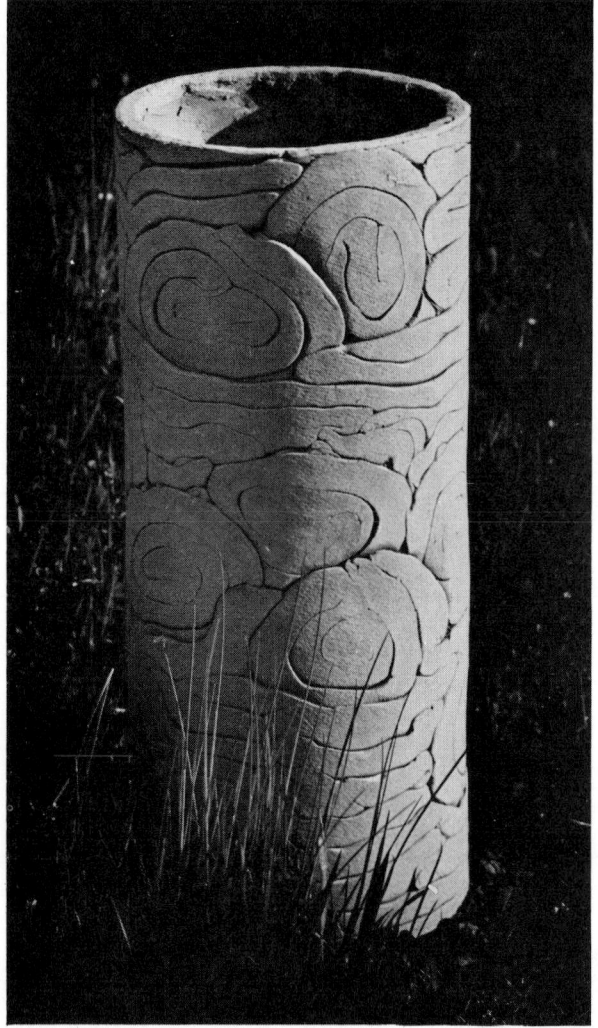

DESIGN: JACK FELTMAN

to plaster or earthenware, but it is necessary to line molds of other materials with strips of newspaper or paper towels, a damp cloth, or plastic wrap. Lining allows the clay to pull away from the mold and prevents cracking. It can be peeled off later.

Line your mold, if necessary. If a cylinder is used, place a slab of clay on the bottom for a base. Using a plastic clay, roll up coils in a variety of patterns. As each module is formed, position along the inside of the mold. Where the patterns meet the base, join the two by pulling clay from pattern to base. Weld adjoining modules by smearing the clay together. (For demonstration purposes and clarity, we've shown our modules being joined *outside* of the mold.) The outer coiled surface of your piece can be left as is or flattened by lightly paddling each module with your hand after joining.

Let the piece dry in the mold until it pulls away from the walls. To remove the cylinder, place a board over the mold opening and invert.

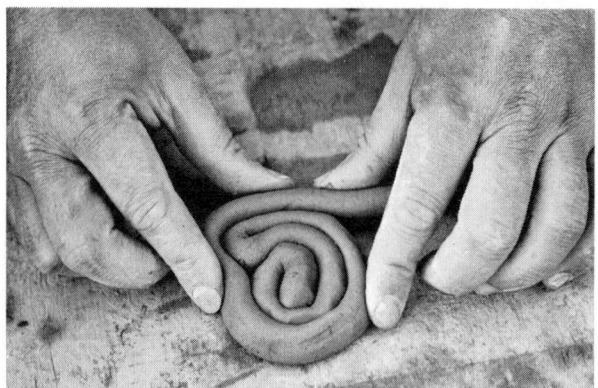

ROLL COILS into modules, place in mold one at a time, join by smearing. (Coils here were joined outside mold for clarity.)

Compared to other methods (such as the wheel where a piece is drawn out of one mass of clay), coiling demands that each coil module be individually formed before construction can begin. Because coiled pieces are built in sections, you have the option of individualizing each part.

Coils can be worked horizontally (see bottle, page 31) or wound up into maze-like pieces and joined (see curled trivet, page 30). If you choose to follow the latter course for anything other than a flat piece, some sort of support is needed. Mixing bowls, earthenware planters, specially made plaster bowls (see plaster, page 15), or cardboard boxes make perfect molds. A cardboard cylinder formerly containing children's blocks was used for this project. Clay won't stick

decorative mirror frame

DESIGN: KAY LINDQUIST

Flat ceramic tiles, the most basic of slab ware, can have a myriad of shapes. This mirror frame is simply a round tile, opened in the center to hold a mirror, decorated by impressing with stamps (see page 63) to emphasize texture.

Although this frame is round, any outline, such as a stylized bird, animal, flower, or freeform can be used. The mirror diameter is governed by the size and shape of mirror available. Inexpensive round cosmetic mirrors are the easiest to find, but the opening can be any shape as long as you plan enough frame-mirror overlap for glueing together. Since the clay will shrink during drying and firing, cut your opening the same size or just smaller than your mirror.

For the frame, prepare a slab ½ to ⅝-inch thick. With a pattern or freehand, use a needle to cut out the outer circumference. Trim away excess clay. Place the mirror in the center of the trimmed slab. Cut around the mirror and remove the center piece. Apply decoration. With a straw or dowel, make two holes near the top of the frame for hanging. Dry the frame slowly and evenly by setting on sticks or placing between thick layers of newspaper. Stain or glaze the frame after it has been bisque fired.

After the final firing, glue (epoxy or silicone adhesive) mirror to frame. To cover the mirror's backside and to protect the wall, glue a piece of felt slightly larger than the diameter of the mirror to the frame.

To hang, use heavy leather lacing — latigo is good. Sueded leather is not strong enough.

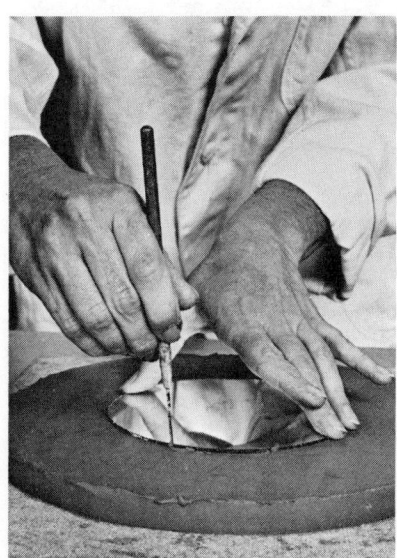 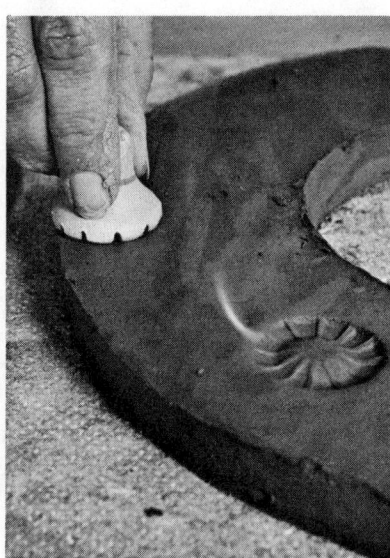 

PLACE MIRROR in center of slab frame and cut out opening (left). Clay will shrink enough so that mirror can be glued onto frame. Decorate frame with stamps (center); with a straw, punch out two holes for hanging (right).

box with hinged lid

Slab-built pieces take on an architectural quality when stiffened, pre-cut squares and rectangles are joined. Partial drying of the slabs before assembling will help to counter warpage, a common problem in slab building. It is essential to firmly seal each joint; otherwise cracks can develop during the firing process. Slab lids can be flanged or, as in this case, attached with hinges. Wood dowels (metal ones can be substituted) just longer than the two hinges were used here to attach the lid to the box.

For a textured inside or outside surface, prepare ½-inch-thick slabs on burlap. Let the slabs dry until they can be moved without bending. On the flattened clay, mark out rectangles for the bottom, the sides, the lid, and the four hinges (see hinge pattern on facing page). Cardboard patterns can be used as cutting guides.

Cut out the pieces with a knife and transfer to a hard, flat working surface. With a fork or other pointed tool, score all joints. Liberally wet scored seams with a sponge and generously coat with slip. Assemble the bottom and sides so that the sides rest on the base, not around it. (If the sides surround the bottom rectangle, the clay may crack as it dries and shrinks.) With a flat stick, paddle all seams well to join securely. Remove excess slip with a scraper.

To attach the upper hinges, measure their placement on the lid. Score both lid and hinges; wet the scoring and apply slip. Fasten on the hinges and paddle. Secure the back hinges in a similar manner, being careful not to get slip in the lid crack or the lid will stick to the box; paddle. With a small wire loop tool or a nail, open a hole in the center of the rounded area of each hinge, carefully lining up the openings of adjoining hinges. Make the opening larger than you need to allow for shrinkage.

A final scraping with a flat edged tool can straighten slightly uneven edges.

Dry the finished piece slowly under plastic as a further check on warpage. It may be helpful to place weights on the lid while drying. For the first and second firings, leave on the lid to coordinate warpage and shrinkage between the top and the box. The box shown was decorated with oxides and glaze. Remember not to glaze the top edges of the box and the underside of the lid or they will fuse together when fired.

See also inside front cover.

DESIGN: PATRICIA SCARLETT

OUTLINE, then cut out pieces from pre-stiffened slabs. Since hinges should match, cut one out and use it as a guide.

WHEN ALL PARTS are ready to assemble, score joints. With sponge, apply water liberally over scored surfaces.

COAT the scored, moistened edges of each part with a generous amount of slip. Slip "glues" the pieces together.

PLACE each wall on the bottom, rather than around it, to prevent the clay from cracking as it dries and shrinks.

PADDLING the seams of the assembled box with a ruler or flat stick will fasten parts together more securely.

SCORE hinge and for upper hinges the lid, for lower hinges the wall. Apply slip to scoring, press hinge to box; paddle to secure.

BORE HOLES in hinges with loop tool or nail. Holes should align and be slightly larger than necessary to allow for shrinkage.

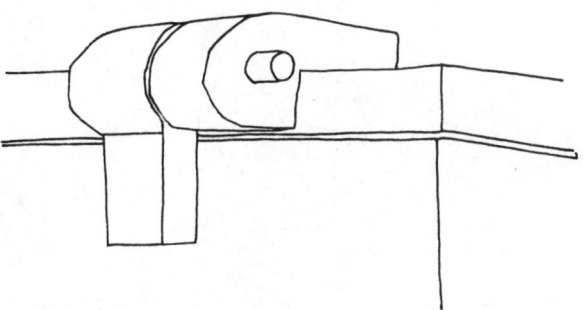

ILLUSTRATION shows how hinges, used in pairs, relate to one another and are secured in place with a wooden dowel.

stoneware buttons

DESIGN: TONI WILLIAMSON

Many clay projects are simple enough to execute in even the smallest working space and with a minimum of tools. Yet limited space and equipment shouldn't stop you from creating attractive and utilitarian objects, such as these handsome buttons.

Stoneware is suggested for this project because of its strength and durability. As an added decorative element, two colors of clay can be incorporated in each button as long as the composition of both clays is the same. As clay shrinks during drying, different types of clay bodies combined in one piece will contract at different rates and may cause a rupture. Stoneware is available ready mixed in several colors or can be tinted with oxides (see page 66).

The bisque-fired buttons were stained with Barnard clay slip which fires brown-black. Iron oxide or manganese dioxide are other stain possibilities. The buttons can also be left as is, although staining will highlight any texture you may incorporate into your design. If you choose to apply a glaze, remember that unless you are able to string the buttons on nichrome wire during the final firing, you should glaze only the top surface. Otherwise, as the glaze melts in the kiln and solidifies, the buttons will fuse to the kiln shelf. This isn't a problem with stains.

Two-color buttons. Prepare two slabs of contrasting color clays, one ¼-inch thick, the other slightly thinner. From the thicker slab, cut out clay discs with a small biscuit cutter, pill container, lipstick tube, or similar sharp-edged device. Punch out as many discs as you need. Transfer the discs to a flat surface (¼-inch-thick plywood is good because the clay won't stick to wood as it dries) by lifting the excess clay away from the buttons, then carefully shifting the discs to the board. From the thinner slab, cut out discs smaller in diameter than the first set. Place one on top of each of the already cut pieces. To firmly join the clays, press down on each button with a stamp (see page 63). Punch out thread holes with a dowel.

Single-color buttons. For a plain surface, cut out discs from ¼-inch-thick slabs, transfer discs to a drying board, and make the thread holes. Remember to make thread holes slightly larger than necessary to allow for shrinkage. For textured buttons, stamp directly onto the slab and cut around the impression.

Note. If the buttons are too thick when dry, sand down with wire mesh, coarse metal sandpaper, or non-woven, webbed kitchen pads.

  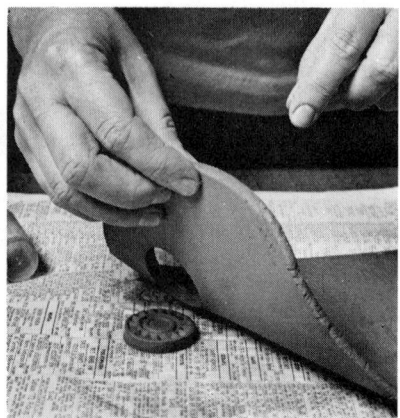

TWO-COLOR BUTTONS are made from circles and rings, each cut from different color clay (left). Lay smaller piece on larger; join with stamp (center). Single-color buttons are stamped and cut directly from one piece of clay (right).

weed holder

See also inside front cover.   DESIGN: JACK FELTMAN

Gently flip the rectangle. Fold the decorated end up and around your hand, leaving about 2 to 3 inches at the top for hanging. With the thumb of your other hand, press down around the edges of the folded slab. Remove your hand. Punch two holes near the upper corners for hanging.

When dry, brush the medallion with iron oxide and sponge off the high spots or leave as is.

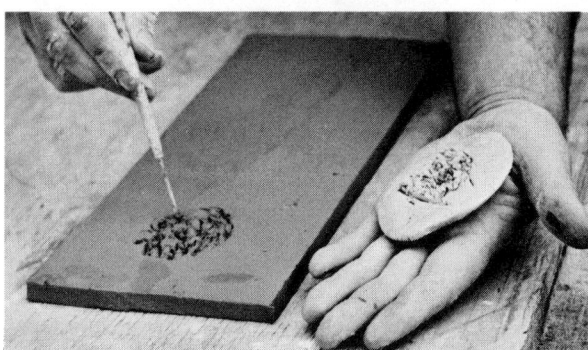

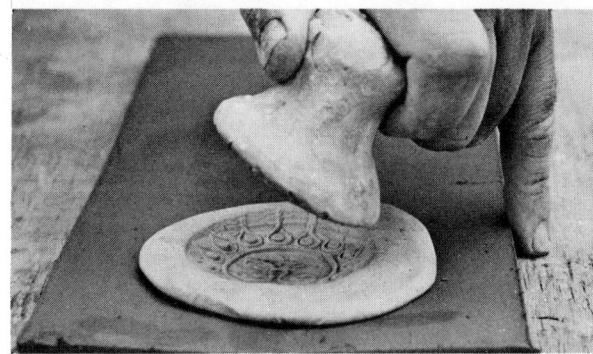

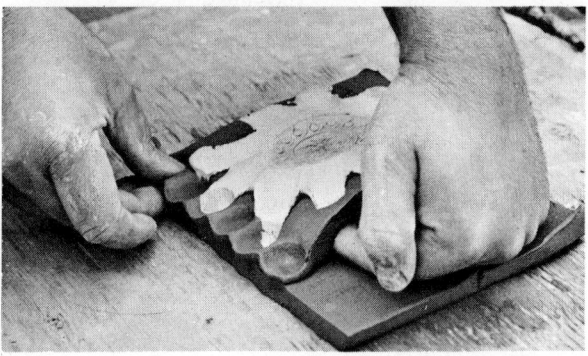

The natural quality of clay is enhanced when the finished piece serves as a foil for other natural materials. For this reason, weed holders are a favorite ceramic project.

This weed holder is made from a rectangular slab and illustrates the ability of plastic clay to be molded around another form — in this case, the potter's hand. Decoration has been kept to a minimum (a medallion of contrasting color clay) to avoid competition with whatever will be displayed in the holder.

From a 1/4-inch-thick slab, cut a rectangle about 12 inches long and 4 1/2 inches wide. The slab could be prepared on burlap to add texture. From another color clay (but of the same composition), shape a flat disc for the medallion. Heavily score one side of the disc and the spot on the slab where the disc will sit. Position the clay disc on the slab and press a stamp (see page 63) firmly into the disc. It may be necessary to moisten the scoring with slip if the clay is not very fresh. With a wiping action of the thumb, pull clay from the edges of the medallion onto the slab. This will further secure disc to slab.

SCORE medallion and slab (top); press together and secure by stamping (middle). Smear edges of disc into slab in regular pattern with thumb. Fold part of slab up and around hand; press along edge with thumb to secure (bottom).

ceramic lanterns

DESIGN: JANE HORN

Let the cylinder stiffen until it can be handled without distorting or is leather hard. After you decide on your surface design, scratch a light outline of the pattern on the cylinder with a needle. Pierce along the outline. Flake off excess clay from the inside. Avoid very small holes or narrow slits, for these will fill up with glaze. A simple dipping in glaze will provide an effective finish, but it may be necessary to carefully clean each light hole free of glaze before firing.

FOR EACH LANTERN, curve a clay rectangle into a cylinder (top). Smooth over seam, then work in a thin coil (middle). Cut a base and attach to cylinder. Outline pattern and pierce (bottom).

The plastic nature of clay permits the hand builder to convert slabs into curved shapes. For this project, a pattern of lightholes has been cut in the walls of a slab cylinder to form a cheerful candleholder, somewhat resembling the tin lanterns of Mexico. Opening the wall of a pot with carved or pierced motifs is another surface treatment you may want to experiment with. It's best to attempt piercing when the clay has stiffened but not dried completely.

As with other "constructed" pieces, secure joints are essential when making a cylinder.

From a 1/4-inch-thick slab, cut out a rectangle which will curve to give you a candleholder of the height and diameter you desire. Form the rectangle into a cylinder, joining the ends in a seam. Trim one end if you wish to adjust the diameter. With a wooden modeling tool or your finger, smooth over the seam by pulling clay across it from both sides. Roll a coil 3/8-inch thick and the height of your cylinder. Press the coil along the seam and model it in to restore an even wall thickness.

On another slab, use the cylinder as a guide to cut out a base. Score the base and the cylinder bottom. Coat the scoring with slip and attach cylinder to base. Smooth over the seam.

freeform wall hanging

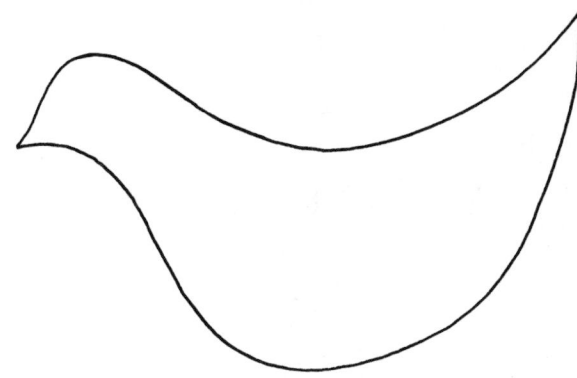

Slabs can be transformed into whimsical plaques, glazed decorative tiles, and planters. This hanging is a fine-feathered bird, but any real or imaginary beast, fish, or fowl will add a gay note to your walls.

Since this hanging is constructed of two duplicate shapes, it's best to use a pattern for cutting accuracy. With a needle and a pattern, cut out the two sides from a slab. Using a wire loop tool, bevel the lower edge of both pieces. On one piece, score the beveling and apply slip. Score the corresponding edge on the *underside* of the other where the two will be attached.

Position a ball of crumpled newspaper in the center of the slab that has both scoring and slip. As you set the other piece over the first, carefully match edges, curves, and corners. With a modeling tool, smooth the seam to make it secure.

When the planter has stiffened or is leather hard, the paper can be removed and decoration applied. Our bird was feathered with the pointed end of an orange stick.

For hanging, determine the center of balance and, on the wall-touching side, punch out two evenly spaced holes and string with leather.

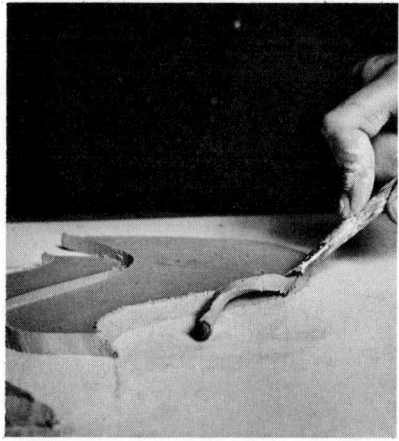 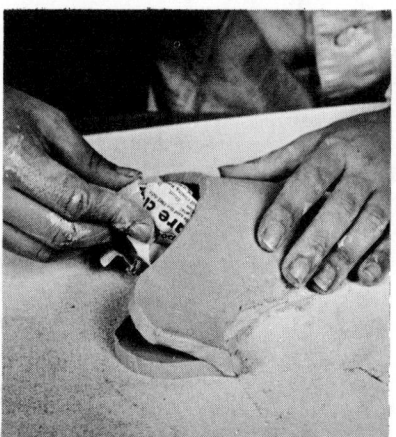 

AFTER CUTTING out front and back pieces of bird from clay slab, bevel lower edges of both pieces so they will fit together smoothly (left). To keep the pieces separated until stiff enough to hold their shape, set a ball of newspaper in center of back part (center) before laying on upper piece. "Feather" bird with any pointed tool (right).

wind chimes

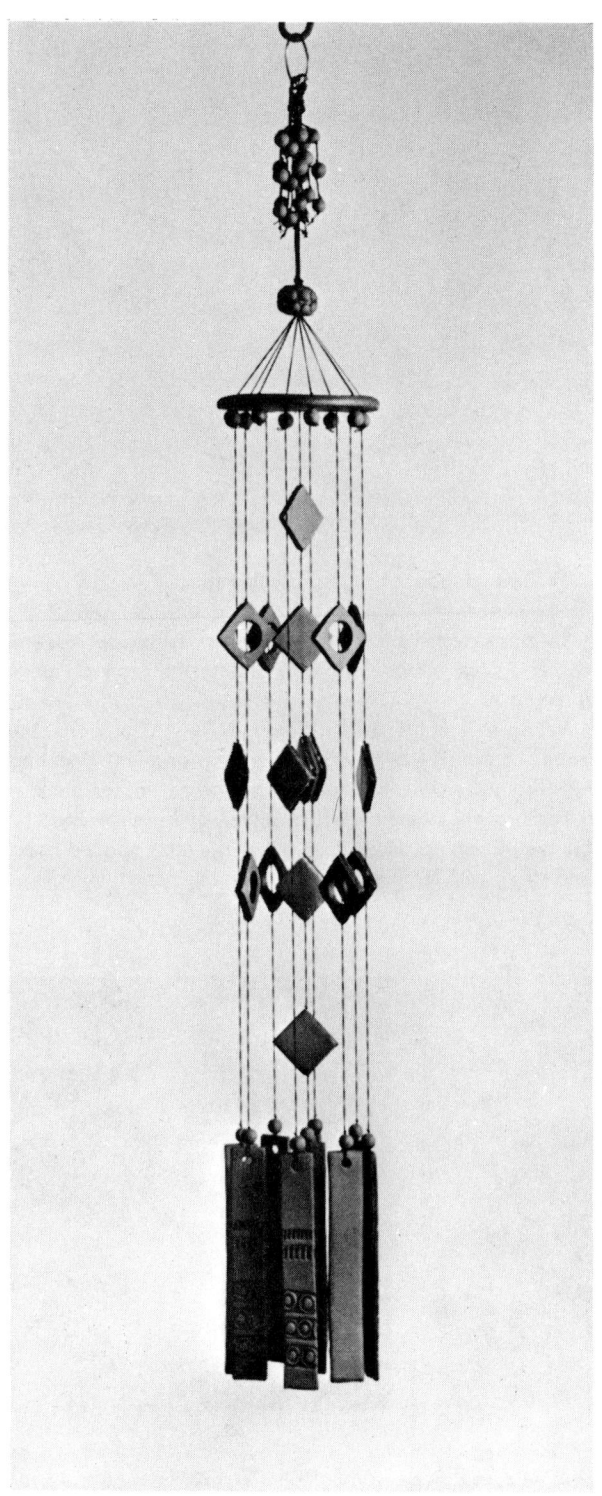

DESIGN: TONI WILLIAMSON

Simple mobiles and wind chimes are excellent projects for children, while more sophisticated designs will challenge the imagination of those potters with a surer mastery of the material.

This particular hanging is an assemblage of decorated bar chimes, slab squares, and beads, portions of which were stained, glazed, or left bare. Thin nylon line or waxed nylon cord of the type used for macrame is good for stringing, since both are fine, yet strong enough to support the clay pieces.

In making wind chimes, remember that the thicker and larger the chime, the more wind is needed to move it. Note that the sound of the chimes may differ, depending on the type of clay you use and whether or not the pieces are glazed. You may want to try several variations of these elements to achieve a tone that pleases you.

Bars. Nine bars are needed as chimes, but it's best to make a few extra of these (and of all the pieces) in case of breakage during the fragile greenware stage.

Prepare several slabs ¼-inch thick. Across the length of one slab, apply decoration. Trim the slab to a rectangle 6 inches wide and 11 inches long (each bar is 1 inch wide by 6 inches long). To avoid distorting the pattern, wait until the slab has stiffened slightly before cutting (use a sharp hobby knife) into eleven 1-inch bars. Punch out stringing holes near the top center of each bar with a straw.

Squares. You will need 17 squares for the design, but make more in case of breakage. Divide another ¼-inch-thick slab into one-inch squares. Punch out a circle in the center of half the squares (you need eight open and nine closed squares). Let stiffen slightly, then separate. With a metal or wood skewer, pierce the squares through from corner to opposite corner or edge to edge. To avoid distortion, pierce the open squares one corner (or one edge) at a time. Be careful to skewer in a straight line to avoid damaging the square.

Beads. From clay scraps, roll at least 17 small beads (about ½ inch in diameter each) and one large bead (about 1½ inches in diameter). Texture large bead, if you wish. Save extra beads to decorate the ends of the threads or for another hanging. Make hole in beads for stringing.

Plate. For the hanging "plate," cut out a 5-inch circle. Around one of the flat sides of the plate, punch out 16 evenly spaced holes and one hole in the center for stringing the chimes together.

To dry. Dry the bars and squares very slowly under plastic, between layers of newspaper, between two thin plaster bats, or on a wire mesh rack. Turn several times very gently during drying. When the pieces are leather hard, they may be smoothed with a damp sponge.

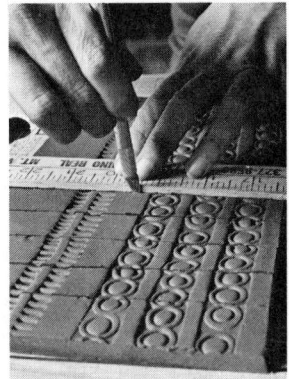

CUT chimes and squares from slightly stiffened rectangles. Pre-texture chimes by stamping slab before cutting.

PIERCE stringing holes in open squares one corner at a time. Make evenly spaced holes in "plate" for stringing.

Stringing the Chimes

Assemble the wind chimes after all the pieces have been given their final firing. Cut nine lengths of cord, 52 inches each. Following the diagram, make four "A" strands, four "B" strands, and one "C" strand. For each strand, insert thread through a bar and pull up until doubled.

Strand "A". Thread a small bead so it sits on top of the bar. Make a knot directly above the bead as follows: loop cord around so that it crosses the double cord just above the bead. Hold the four threads where they meet with your fingers and bring the free ends through the loop from underneath. Work the knot very slowly to keep it next to the bead (see knotting diagram far right). To string the first square, go 6 inches from the top of the bar, knot. Thread one open square and knot again. Make another knot 12½ inches from the bar. Add another open square; knot. Repeat for remaining three "A" strands.

Strand "B". Thread a small bead so it sits on top of the bar, as in Strand A; knot. Make the next knot 9 inches from the bar; add a closed square; knot. Repeat for remaining three "B" strands.

Strand "C". Thread a small bead so it sits on top of the bar, as in strands A and B; knot. Make a knot 1¾ inches from the bar; attach a closed square; knot. The succeeding knots will be 6, 9, 12½ and 15¾ inches from the bar. After each knot, attach a closed square and knot again to hold the square in place.

To attach to top. Measure all nine strands to ensure that lengths match. Strand "C" will probably be the shortest because of all the knots used, so measure it first by stretching it to straighten and then letting it hang loose. Adjust the remaining strands to the length of Strand "C".

For each strand, insert the double threads through a hole in the plate. "C" hangs in the center and "A" and "B" alternate around the edge. Remember to thread every other hole. Pull the thread through up to the top square to even the cord. Make a knot at the end of the string, then let it fall. If you wish, dab glue on each knot to hold the strand secure.

For hanging, cut eight 44-inch strands. Double each strand. At looped end of each doubled strand, tie a knot. Thread a small bead and knot again. Insert a beaded thread through each of the remaining holes in the plate with the bead on the underside of the plate; knot above and close to the plate. When all threads are in the plate, thread them through the large bead, which sits approximately 3 inches above the plate. Knot on top of the large bead.

These chimes were hung with 14-gauge brass wire. (A curtain ring will do also.) Cut the wire about 8 inches long. Make double loops at each end of the wire for better securing. Curve into a ring.

Separate thread ends. Thread 8 through the ring from the left and 8 through from the right. Tie one square knot below the ring and secure with 2 overhand knots.

Beads can be threaded onto the ends of the 8 doubled threads for added decoration.

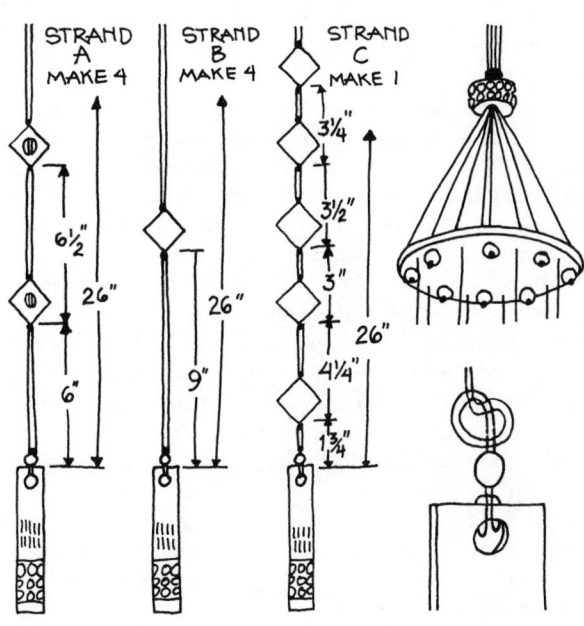

name plaque

DESIGN: KAY LINDQUIST

abcdefg
hijklmn
opqrstu
vwxyz
1234567
890

Slabs can be used intact or regarded as a material out of which you can create smaller shapes. For example, this name plaque uses ceramic letters cut from a slab, glazed, and glued to driftwood. Other possibilities are slab medallions and mobiles.

The alphabet given here was used for this plaque. Newspaper type is another source for interesting letters. Or, design your own. Have the newspaper page or a tracing photostated and enlarged to whatever size you need. From the sample, prepare stencil paper patterns to serve as cutting guides.

The glazed letters (or numbers) can be glued with epoxy or a silicone adhesive to almost any hard surface. Wood (not bark, for it peels) or shingles make attractive backgrounds for the letters, as do fences, doors, and walls. If the plaque is to hang outdoors, you should glue the letters or numbers with a waterproof glue.

On a 3/8-inch-thick slab, arrange letters cut from heavy paper. Leave enough space between letters to easily remove excess clay. With a smooth motion and a needle, cut around each letter. Then, with the needle, carefully lift up and remove the extra clay without disturbing the letters. Gently peel off the patterns. Wait until the letters are leather hard before smoothing the edges so that they will not lose their sharpness.

Brush glaze onto the top surface of the bisqued letters. If you are making a plaque, use a saw tooth picture hanger (available at home building supply centers or hardware stores) for even hanging.

USE needle to cut around each letter (top). Cut away excess clay (bottom); lift up and remove excess with needle. Peel off patterns; let letters stiffen before smoothing to keep letters sharp.

plate made on a mold

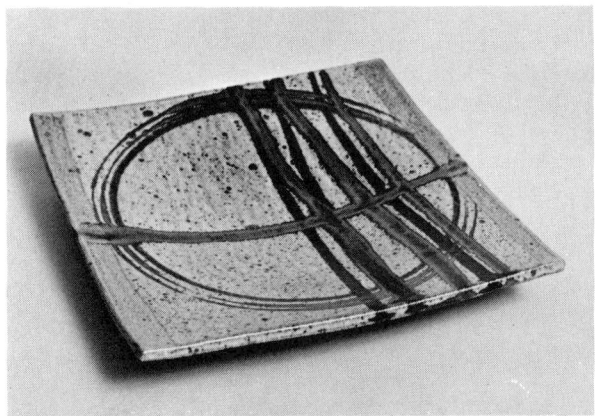

DESIGN: ERIC NORSTAD

Footed plates are easy to make off the wheel by draping a slab over a mold. The mold can be one of many materials: a smooth hump of plaster; a solid lump of dried clay which has been covered with a damp cloth, paper towel, or plastic wrap to prevent sticking; styrofoam cut to whatever shape you want; or a large flat rock.

The foot can be made from a coil, slab strip, several plugs of clay (three rather than four feet provide the most stability), or it can be thrown on the wheel. The foot is joined to the plate while the plate is still on the mold and when the piece is stiff enough to handle without distorting. After the foot is attached, it will need time to stiffen to support the plate, so coordinate foot and plate drying time. Remember that the drying clay will shrink around the non-shrinking mold. If the plate is not removed before being completely dry, the piece will crack.

Decorate when the plate is leather hard or after the first firing. This plate's pattern was created by brushing oxides over slip, then glazing.

Prepare a slab about $\frac{1}{4}$ to $\frac{3}{8}$-inch thick on a piece of cloth. Place slightly stiffened slab over mold or lift the cloth and invert the clay onto the mold. Make sure the slab fits tightly across its whole surface. Trim the clay to the shape you want.

Decide the type of foot that best complements your plate. Score plate and foot, then apply slip to scoring and weld with a modeling tool. Some potters leave the indentation from modeling; others add a thin coil around the joint, which is then smoothed over. (A coil smoothed into a joint will always add strength.)

As soon as the plate is stiff enough to move, remove the mold. Edges can be further trimmed or finished with a damp sponge.

If the plate is to be used for food, it's best not to texture the surface because food will catch in the grooves, making cleaning difficult.

Dry slowly under plastic.

POSITION slab over mold so that all points touch mold's surface. Burlap will texture clay and prevent slab from sticking to mold. Trim the slab to desired shape with a needle tool.

WHILE PLATE is still on mold, attach foot. Work thin coil into smoothed joint for added strength. Tool marks can be left for decoration (as they were here) or smoothed over.

jewelry and beads

BEADS and pendants can be pinched, made from coils, or cut from slabs. Leather was used to string beads.

Scraps of clay can be recycled into handsome beads and pendants for use in making jewelry, wall hangings, room dividers, or buttons. They can also become an integral part of woven or knotted designs.

Because of their small size, there is always room for beads during a bisque firing. Make beads often, even if you have no immediate project in mind, for the more beads you have available when you begin stringing, the greater the creative possibilities.

Any hand-building technique is suitable for beadwork. For pinched beads, flatten pieces of clay with your fingers or roll into balls. Thick coils of clay sliced with a sharp knife make attractive "filler" tubes for necklaces or hangings. Almost any shape medallion can be cut from a slab.

Use several types of beads in a single piece for a more visually pleasing effect.

Bore holes for stringing when the clay has stiffened slightly so as not to push the bead out of shape. The size of the hole depends upon what you plan to use to string the beads. Keep in mind that both bead and hole will shrink during drying and firing, so make the holes slightly larger than you need. Thin nylon fishing line, macrame cords, heavy twine, and leather strips are all suitable stringing materials. Avoid cord that will fray from the friction of the moving beads. A knot between every bead keeps them fixed in place. (See wind chimes, page 40, for a discussion of knotting.)

Texture beads by leaving a rough surface when shaping, pressing on or between textured surfaces, or marking the clay with whatever makes a pleasing impression.

If you glaze your beads, they must be strung on ni-

chrome wire (available at any ceramic supply store) so that they will not stick to the kiln shelf. To avoid this problem, stain the pieces with an oxide to bring out texture or form your beads from different color clays. When designing with beads, consider the final use of the piece. A large, heavy bead may work well in a wall hanging but would be very uncomfortable to wear.

HANGING is combination of 1) porcelain tubes and beads; 2) stoneware tubes, beads, and stamped discs strung together. Porcelain is left bare, some stoneware is stained to bring out texture (see inside front cover for necklace made in same manner).

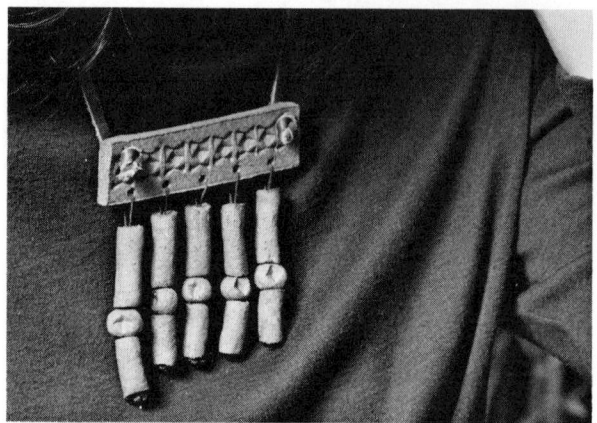

ATTRACTIVE and simple necklace utilizes leftover clay. Clay tubes and beads were strung to textured rectangle.

additional hand-building ideas

The pieces on this and the next two pages are further examples of the potter's ingenuity in developing forms without using the wheel. They run the gamut from the attractively utilitarian (the striking tiled bath), to the strictly for fun (the imaginative and delightful ceramic houses and the free-fall ''Sky Pilot''). Whatever course you choose to follow with clay, remember that the final product will be something very special, a personal expression of your own creativity.

DRAMATICALLY DECORATED with slip and oxide, this coil-built, lidded jar illustrates the versatility of coil method.

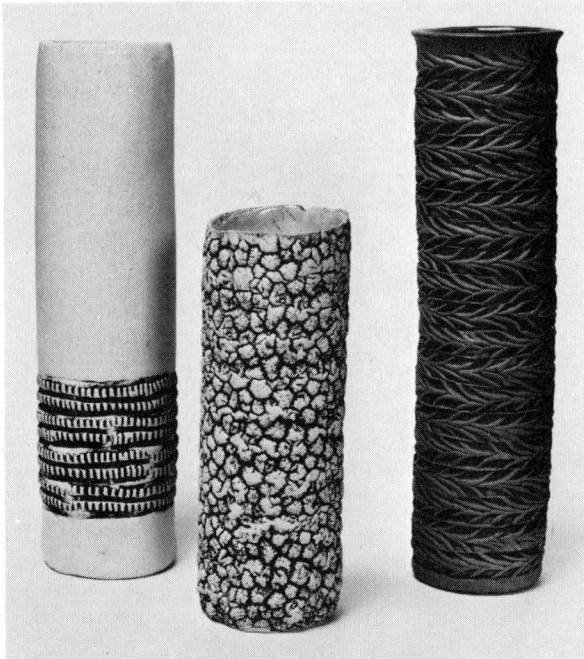

VASES are pre-textured slabs, shaped by being wrapped around a rolling pin. Staining highlights stamped texture.

NAPKIN RINGS can be clay strips pulled like a pulled handle or cut from a slab. Here, incising decorates joins.

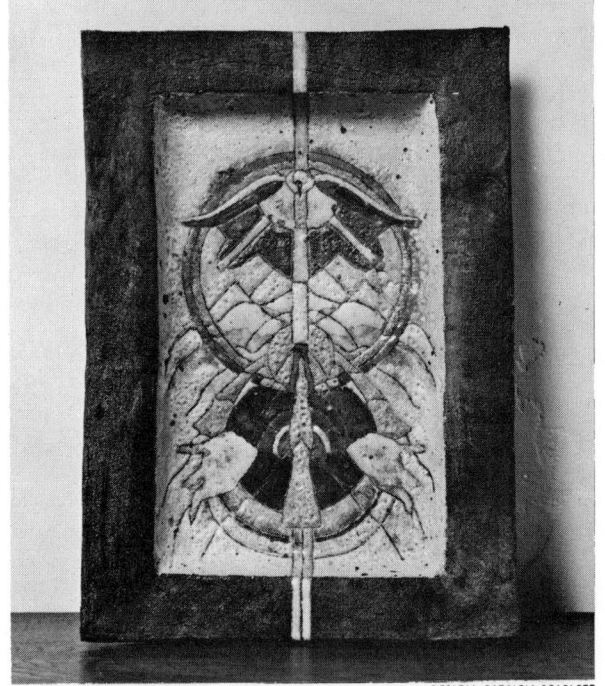

RELIGIOUS in feeling, intricate pattern on molded slab stoneware tray was created with oxides and glaze.

COLORFUL low-fire glazes over low-fire clays highlight dwelling. Note overturned garbage can, sleeping dog, car on blocks.

DESIGN: CAROLINE HARMON

DESIGN: TONI WILLIAMSON

CLAY MUSHROOM cutouts were arranged in mold first, then coils were positioned in the mold to form stoneware bowl.

DESIGN: RUTH DUCKWORTH; ANTONIO PRIETO COLLECTION OF CERAMICS, MILLS COLLEGE

POWERFUL SLAB-CONSTRUCTED stoneware form utilizes rough, bare surface of clay as a decorative element.

TEXTURED SURFACE of large coiled planter is result of impressions made by tool (a pencil) used to join coils.

DESIGN: VIKTORIA CHULAY

DESIGN: DEBBY MANFREE

FANCIFUL COTTAGE was hand built with great attention to detail—sloping roof, stone chimney, paned windows, shutters.

DESIGN: RON COOPER

CONTEMPORARY "free-falling" sky pilot was sculptured out of low-fire clays and decorated with colorful low-fire glazes.

DESIGN: REESE BULLEN; ANTONIO PRIETO COLLECTION OF CERAMICS, MILLS COLLEGE

INSPIRATION for stoneware sack was paper satchel. Oxides and glaze were brushed on in abstract pattern.

DESIGN: KAY LINDQUIST

BALLOON was used for mold to form body of glazed stoneware pig. Ears, coiled tail, feet were shaped, then added.

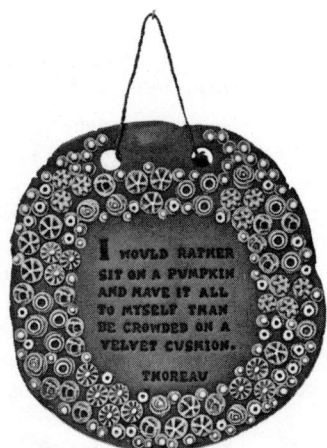

DESIGN: TONI WILLIAMSON

MOTTO was impressed with uncooked alphabet noodles, then stained. Various stamps decorate perimeter of plaque.

DESIGN: MARILYN MAC KENZIE

INDIVIDUAL ceramic tiles were formed, then set in place to create bold geometric designs around bath area.

Working
on the potter's wheel

Working on the potter's wheel looks deceptively simple to the novice as he watches a potter quickly and gracefully draw out a symmetrical, open form from a ball of clay. Actually, throwing requires expert instruction, study, practice, and a great deal of skill. The best way to learn to throw is under the guidance of another potter who can watch as you work, correcting problems as they occur, and by observing other potters in action.

Consequently, this chapter, intended only as a general introduction to working on the wheel, is approached somewhat differently than the section on hand building. Step-by-step instructions for the throwing techniques are given; however, step-by-step projects are not included. Several pages at the end of this chapter show a variety of thrown ware to give you an idea of what can be accomplished with practice and imagination.

For each of the basic throwing techniques included, we demonstrate one method of approach. But, as is true with all aspects of ceramics, the best method is the one that works for you.

Types of wheels. Although many types of wheels are available, basically they fall into two categories: kick wheels (those powered by the potter's foot) and electrically driven wheels. Each has its advantages. If you learn on the kick wheel, you become familiar with the throwing process by having to use your whole body. At the same time, you are developing hand-foot coordination. Kick wheels are quieter and generally less expensive than electric wheels of comparable quality.

An electric wheel is usually smaller and lighter than a kick wheel. You can learn more quickly on it because, not having to worry about keeping the wheel turning with your foot, you can give full attention to your hand movements. And, since much of the work is done by the wheel, the potter can channel more energy into making pots. Electric wheels are a boon to the production potter who must turn out many pieces quickly.

Most likely you'll learn to throw in a classroom situation or be taught by a friend on his wheel. If you decide that you want your own wheel, consider the following factors. Wheels range in cost from about $50 for a kick wheel kit

DESIGN: BONNIE IKEMURA

SWIRLS of oxide and glaze complement very symmetrical lines of wheel-thrown bowl (see also inside back cover).

(just the metal parts, you have to build the frame) to $400 or more for the best power wheels with variable speeds. How much room can you allot to a wheel? Kick wheels generally need more space than electric wheels. In addition, if you like to work on the wheel after a day on the job, a sit-down kick wheel (stand-up wheels take less energy) may require more energy than you have left at the end of the day.

The type of wheel you choose may be the kind on which you learned. You will have had experience in using that particular model and will feel confident working on it.

Whatever you decide, don't make a hasty purchase. Read the literature and specification sheets available from manufacturers and ceramic supply stores, talk to other potters, and try out as many models as you can.

Type of clay. Once you're at a wheel — in your home, classroom, or elsewhere — you're ready to start. The type of clay used for wheel work varies from potter to potter, depending on personal preference. Generally, throwing clay should be plastic enough for easy handling, yet be able to retain its shape. Beginners often produce pots that slump from overworking. A clay with grog (anywhere from 10 to 20 percent) will hold up better than one with no grog at all, although the more grog it contains, the less plastic the clay will be. Try several clays until you find one that suits your needs.

Clay must be thoroughly wedged for throwing (see wedging, page 12). Wedging will remove air pockets that may distort the walls as you work, helps line up the clay particles, and homogenizes moisture content.

centering the clay

Before any shape can be developed on the wheel, the clay must rest in the very center of the wheel head. The centering process develops a mound of clay that will spin on the same axis as the wheel. Working from an uncentered mound will result in wobbly walls, not uniformly thick. Since symmetry is the hallmark of wheel-thrown pots, uneven walls are aesthetically undesirable. Irregularities in wall thickness could present problems later on, such as warping, cracking, or explosions during firing. Finally, it would be difficult to trim a foot on an uncentered pot.

Thrown pieces can be made directly on the wheel or on a bat (see page 15). Most potters prefer to use a bat; this allows you to set aside a piece that needs to stiffen before it can be worked further, prevents possible distortion when removing a newly formed piece from the wheel prematurely, and frees the wheel for another project.

Have all your tools within easy reach before you start. You will need a natural sponge, a basin of water, a needle tool, and, if you are working directly on the wheel head, a wire, nylon cord, or string to cut the pot off.

To center the clay. Initially, both your hands and the throwing clay must be completely dry or the clay won't adhere to the throwing surface. Pat the clay into a ball (its size depends on the size of the finished piece). Using your eye or the concentric rings inscribed on the wheel head, determine the center of the throwing surface, then slam the clay ball onto that spot. Slap the ball down around its sides into a cone-shaped mound for better adhesion.

Rotate the wheel counterclockwise as fast as possible and, with a sponge, squeeze water over the mound until it glistens. Wet your hands also. Because water acts as a lubricant, keep hands and the clay surface consistently moist throughout all stages of throwing.

To firmly support your hands, brace your elbows against your sides, on your knees, or on the wheel frame. With the wheel turning at high speed, place your hands around the far side of the mound and pull against the clay towards the center and up the mound. This action forces the uneven, lumpy clay surface upward until it is deposited on the top.

Then place your thumbs on the top of the cone, hands clasped around the clay, and push down, first using your thumbs and then letting your hands continue down the sides to control the clay as it flares from downward pressure. Repeat the drawing up and pushing down several times.

With practice, you will be able to tell by touch if your clay is centered. Another way is to hold a needle lightly against the mound sides and slowly spin the wheel. If concentric rings of the same depth appear, the clay is centered. Or hold your index finger about $1/2$ inch from the mound and rotate the wheel. If the distance between your finger and the mound is constant, the clay is centered.

To prepare the centered mound for opening, flatten the surface by pressing down on top of the cone with the flat of one hand; pull in against the side with the other.

1) SLAP clay ball into cone with hands.

2) PULL wet clay towards center and up.

3) MOVE clay to top of mound to form cone.

4) PUSH down with thumbs, in with hands.

5) USE NEEDLE to see if clay is centered.

6) FLATTEN mound before opening.

forming a cylinder

GRACEFUL wheel-thrown cylinder has pebbled, "orange peel" surface typical of salt-glazed ware.

DESIGN: TIM MATHER

After the clay is centered, you are ready to open the mound. The shape of the opening, or well, will be determined by the shape of the piece to be thrown. Generally, a cylinder has a flat, interior bottom, and a bowl has a curved one.

Since the cylinder is the basic form from which other shapes are developed and is the most difficult to do, it should be mastered first. Practice throwing as many cylinders as you can, as tall and as even as possible. Study their shape in cross section to analyze wall thickness and form.

To open the centered mound (and for all subsequent stages in the throwing process), have the wheel spinning just slightly slower than for centering. Make sure your forearms are well supported. Since the well should be exactly in the center to develop uniform walls, position the working thumb over the center of the mound. Brace that thumb with your other thumb to allow a true vertical drop into the clay. The fingers of the bracing hand must be resting on the mound sides. Plunge the thumb into the clay to within $\frac{1}{2}$ to $\frac{3}{4}$ inch of the base. Test for base thickness with a needle. If the base is too thick, repeat the procedure until you have the desired depth.

To open the well, keep the outside hand stable by resting it on the clay and insert the thumb of the other hand into the base. Pull away from your body with that thumb until you have the desired diameter.

To pull up the cylinder, place the fingers of the left hand at the base of the inside. Then, with the right hand, apply pressure at the base of the outside so that a ledge is formed. Then move the right hand up until it is opposite the left, and, with one fluid motion, pull the clay completely up to the top of the wall.

Keep the fingers of both hands equally distant and maintain even pressure all the way up to avoid overly thinning the upper walls.

If the top flares out, restore a true vertical by constricting the walls with your hands starting at the bottom and riding up to the top.

Repeat the pulling up process several times to get the walls as thin (about $\frac{1}{4}$ inch) as possible. If the rim is uneven, insert a needle into the wall and slowly rotate the pot until you've cut off a ring of clay.

To form a lip at the top edge, leave enough thickness to work with. Stabilize the wall with the fingers of one hand and press gently along the rim with the index finger of the other hand. You can also use a piece of sponge, chamois, or folded paper.

If you wish to make a narrow neck, gradually constrict the clay to the desired diameter. You must begin exerting pressure well below where the neck will begin.

The outside of the cylinder can be smoothed further with a small-pored sponge. If the cylinder was made directly on the wheel, cut it from the wheel with a wire and lift or gently slide onto a bat to dry. If the cylinder was thrown on a bat, remove the bat. Let the cylinder dry on the bat but cut between the bottom of the cylinder and the bat to prevent the clay from cracking. When the piece is leather hard, trim away excess clay with a knife or needle, then invert and finish trimming (see trimming, page 56).

CROSS SECTION shows evenness of form, thickness of wall.

1) TO OPEN, plunge thumb to within ½ to ¾ inch of base.

2) TO FORM WELL, pull clay away from body with thumb.

3) TO PULL up cylinder, first form ledge on outside base.

4) PULL CLAY up in one motion, maintaining even pressure.

5) RESTORE vertical walls, if necessary, by constricting.

6) FORM LIP by pressing gently with index finger.

forming a bowl

A BOWL is an easier shape to throw than a cylinder. This one is made of stoneware, decorated with glaze.

STUDY your first few weeks' efforts in cross section to note progress in developing an even shape.

You must be careful to create a smooth upward curve, or the bowl may collapse. If you pay particular attention to developing the interior line of your bowl, the outside will follow naturally. As with the cylinder, throw many bowls and study your progress.

The initial steps for centering the clay for a bowl are the same as those used for the cylinder, except that the flattened mound is apt to be wider in proportion to its height. To open the centered mound, you might try the two-thumb method shown in step 1.

Test for base thickness with a needle tool.

The first step in forming the bowl is to pull the clay up into a low cylinder. The walls are thicker here than at the corresponding stage for a taller cylinder because extra clay is necessary for flaring.

Since the bowl is basically a weak shape, it is important not to overwork the walls. Try to form the lip as much as possible before pulling out the walls.

To flare the walls, position the left hand inside the well at the center and the right hand at the outside base. In a continuous motion, move the left hand to the wall and up to the top, exerting pressure to force the wall to spread. The right hand, resting on the outside of the wall, follows the left hand to support and control this motion.

The flare is gradually developed over several movements. If you attempt to pull it all out at once, the clay may be stretched too quickly and crack. You can use a sponge to remove excess water that may weaken the walls.

When you're satisfied with the shape, finish the lip.

Newly thrown bowls and plates are very fragile and should sit on the wheel or bat to stiffen. You take the chance of deforming the wet clay if you attempt to remove it at this stage. When the piece is leather hard, trim it (see page 56).

1) OPEN centered mound with two-thumb method.

2) INSERT needle into base to check for desired thickness.

3) TO FORM BOWL, first pull clay up into low cylinder.

4) CONTINUE shaping cylinder until you have desired height.

5) FORM LIP before flaring walls to avoid distortion.

6) FLARE WALLS with left hand, support with right.

7) DEVELOP FLARE gradually over several movements.

8) AS A FINAL STEP, finish shaping the lip.

working off the mound

DESIGN: JACK FELTMAN

THROWING off a mound of clay can save time. You produce finished shapes that need little or no trimming.

An alternative to working directly on the wheel or on a bat is to throw from a large centered clay cone that rests on the wheel head. This is an excellent, fast method for producing small, repetitive shapes because you don't have to repeat the centering process for each piece. Since every piece is immediately cut off after it is thrown, you save work space by not having to allow one drying bat per pot.

Throwing off the mound allows for an economical use of clay. Because you work right down to the wheel, you'll have only minor waste and few scraps to be discarded or re-worked. Further, as the clay mound gives under pressure, functioning almost as a flexible bat, the potter can cut under his piece at the bottom, producing pots that are generally finished as they come off. Little or no trimming is necessary. Finally, because you are working on a raised surface, you are able better to evaluate the total form, including the inward curves of the outside lower walls.

Traditionally, about 25 pounds of clay are worked into one mound. Although you must center more often, some potters feel that less time and energy in centering is expended by working with half that amount.

To start, draw the centered clay up into a cone and flatten the top. Compact the clay at the top into as close the configuration of the final piece as possible. For example, a vertical piece should be pulled from a vertically shaped thin cone. Make a definite indentation by constricting the clay with your hands where the base of your pot will be. If you remember to cut off your pot below this registration point, you won't be slicing through the bottom of the piece.

Then, open and shape your pot. (The potter here is throwing one of the small bottles pictured above.) To develop and finish the lower curve, exert pressure from an angled tool at the base of the pot.

Cut your piece off the mound by pulling under the base with a length of string wrapped around the far side of the pot and crossed over at the front. To remove the freed pot from the mound, make a "v" with the index and middle fingers of each hand and gently grasp the base at opposite sides. Lift the pot up and off.

1) SHAPE top into form outline.

2) INDENT clay below base.

3) OPEN cone and shape.

4) FORM lower curve with tool.

5) CUT from mound with string.

6) LIFT pot off with fingers.

Lid Made off the Mound

Throwing off the mound allows you to trim the base of your piece while it is right side up. This works particularly well when making certain types of lids, for you can shape a base on the lid that will project into the jar to hold the lid securely in place.

Throw the jar first. Measure the jar with calipers to determine the width of the lid. Remove the jar from the mound.

Pull up the mound into a cone. Flatten the top, then form a solid, squat bottle shape.

Pull out the lid from the bulge of the bottle with an outward and upward lifting movement.

Shape the knob from the neck of the bottle.

Cut a curve with an angled tool for the lid's base; this will hold it in place in the jar.

Measure the lid's diameter to make sure it matches the opening of the jar. Cut off the mound.

POT AND LID were thrown off a mound of clay. Lid has a projecting base that keeps it in place.

1) MAKE a squat bottle shape from the flattened cone.

2) FORM LID from bottle's bulge, knob from neck.

3) CUT in below lid to make projecting base.

4) COMPARE lid size to jar opening before cutting off.

trimming your pot

After your pot has been formed, excess clay at the base usually must be removed. Most often, a foot is carved out of the base of a thrown pot as a finishing touch and to provide a platform for the pot to stand on. Some potters prefer to trim only the lower walls, leaving the bottom flat.

Trimming is done when the pot is leather hard. If attempted too soon, the shape of the pot can be distorted. If the pot is too dry, it can't be carved. Some of the clay can be cut off with a knife or a needle before the pot is inverted for final trimming. Be very careful not to cut away too much.

Place the pot, rim down, on the center of the wheel. Secure the pot to the wheel by pressing pieces of moist clay at several points around the rim. If the pot has a narrow neck, use a chuck (see equipment, page 15). Make sure that the piece is centered by testing with your finger tip (see page 49). Keep in mind the thickness of the lower wall and base as you work so you know how much clay can be removed without cutting through the pot.

Use a wire loop tool for trimming. The hand that holds the tool must be supported both by its forearm (rest against your body or against the wheel frame) and by the other hand. Note that the thumb of the left hand, acting as a brace for the finger controlling the tool, rests on the pot to feel for any irregularities as you trim.

Turn the wheel moderately fast. Lay the tool against the pot where you want to begin trimming. With the tool as steady and secure as possible (to avoid gouging), trim away thin strips of clay. If too much clay is pulled off at one time, the pot can slide off the wheel. Develop the contour gradually until you have taken off as much clay as you want or until you reach the point at which you want to make the foot rim.

To open the foot, place the tool in the center. With the wheel in motion, pull the tool out to the side until you have the desired rim thickness. Then refine this basic outline by first finishing the foot opening and then returning to the outer wall.

Stop at various stages as you trim to check for base thickness. Stop trimming if the base depresses when tapped or if it produces a hollow sound when thumped. Remove sharp edges with a damp sponge or by holding your thumb over the edges while the wheel is in motion.

1) FASTEN pot to be trimmed to wheel with lumps of clay.

2) HOLDING the tool steady, trim away thin strips of clay.

3) TRIM to desired shape or to where foot rim will begin.

4) OPEN the foot by trimming clay from the center out.

spouts, lids, handles

Aside from trimming a foot, you may want to make other modifications to the basic shape of your pot. (For additional spout, lid, and handle ideas, see page 25.)

Spouts. Construction of spouts for thrown pieces depends upon the nature of each piece. A spout for a pitcher is pulled while the clay is still plastic (see page 25). Tea pot spouts are thrown from a cylinder that is narrowed at the top in a process that is much like shaping a neck. When stiff, the spout is cut off at a diagonal from its base, scored, and attached to the leather-hard pot which is scored and covered with slip. Before positioning the spout on the pot, bore several straining holes within the area where the spout will sit. For extra strength at the joint and a smoother transition from spout to pot, weld in a thin coil of clay.

Lids for wheel-thrown pots should be made on the wheel. See page 55 for directions for throwing a set-in lid. Although it is thrown off the mound, the lid can be adapted to working on a bat. Following are several ways a lid relates to its base.

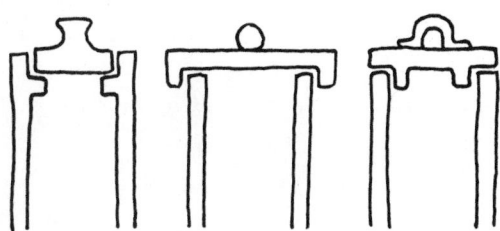

Handles can be made in a variety of ways. To make several handles at once, throw a cylinder and cut off rings of varying widths. Slice open the ring at one point to make one long handle or cut the ring in half for two short ones.

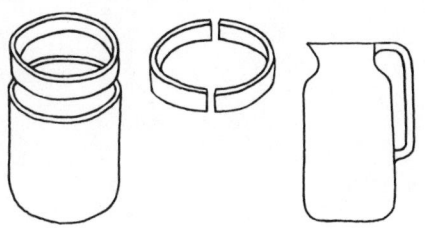

Pulled Handle

The pulled handle is one that complements the fluid lines of a wheel-thrown pot. Hold a well-wedged, pear-shaped wad of clay with one hand. Wet the other hand and grasp the bottom section of the clay and pull down, squeezing as you pull. Gradually lengthen the handle by pulling downward gently several times.

Shape the length of clay during the last few pulls by stroking downward with the thumb and forefinger held against the clay and on opposite sides of it.

Bend the handle into shape and let stiffen. Cut the handle free from the lump of clay at the top and attach to the pot. Score and apply slip to the areas to be joined.

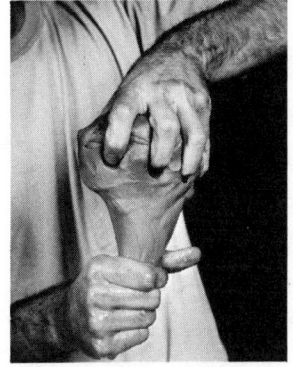 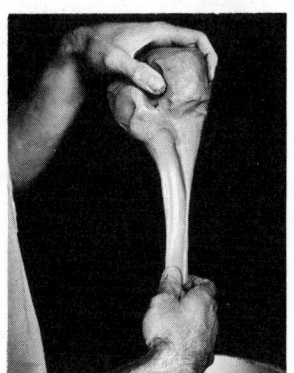

Slab Pulled Handle

A handle that resembles a pulled handle can be made from a slab strip. Cut a strip of clay about 3/8-inch thick and as long as you need. Wet the strip well with a sponge. Position your thumbs on the top of the strip on either side of its center. Press slightly into the clay and, maintaining even pressure, draw the thumbs along the entire length of the strip. Shape it into whatever style handle is needed.

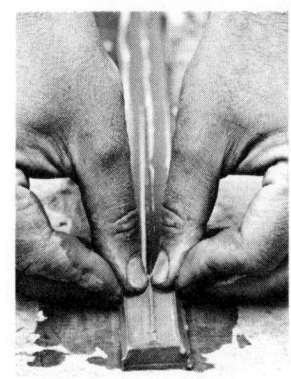 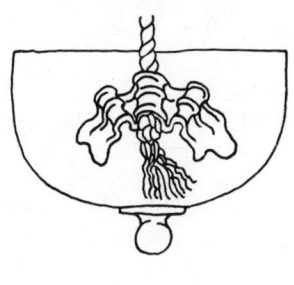

ideas for wheel-thrown projects

Compared to hand building, working on the potter's wheel requires more time and energy to acquire the basic skills. With practice, though, you will be able to take a simple shape, such as a cylinder or bowl, and transform it into a unique object. The variety of wheel-thrown pieces shown here illustrate what can be created with mastery over techniques and much imagination.

DESIGN: ELIZABETH HEIL

THROWN CASSEROLE with lid has earthy-brown glaze, slip "feathers," brightly glazed comb (see also front cover).

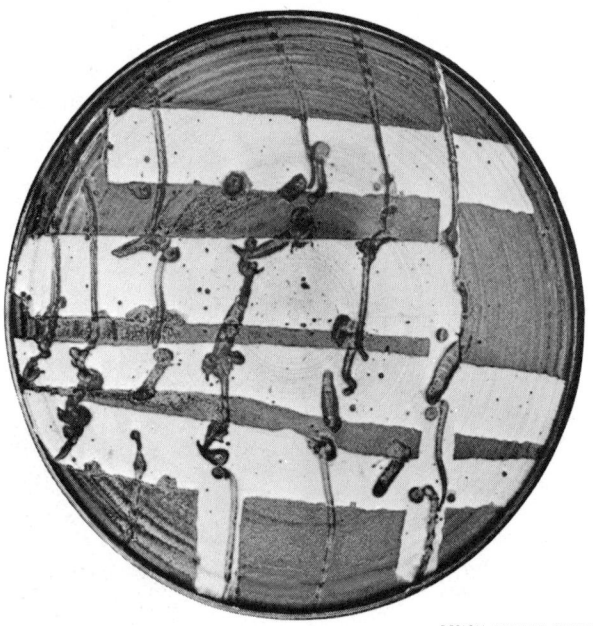

DESIGN: WILLIAM CREITZ

STONEWARE BOWL, 22 inches in diameter, is decorated with ash glaze brushed over blue, white, and brown slip.

DESIGN: DIANA LEON

SPICE JARS and canisters are an attractive combination of bare clay, partial glazing, stamping, and staining.

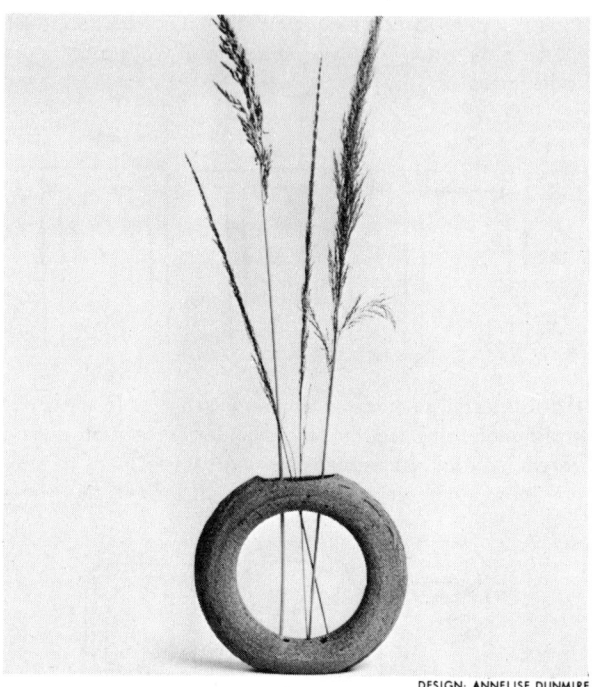

DESIGN: ANNELISE DUNMIRE

THROW a low bowl, open it in the center, pull the walls up and in forming a closed ring, to make this weed holder.

DESIGN: ERIC NORSTAD

STRONG LINES of stoneware tureen are emphasized by the restrained use of brushed and incised decoration.

DESIGN: MARILYN MAC KENZIE

THROWN AND MULTI-GLAZED stoneware mug has sturdy and unusual alligator base, looped coiled handle.

DESIGN: CHARLES COUNTS

ROUGH, UNGLAZED surface of rounded stoneware teapot is a major design element (see also inside back cover).

DESIGN: LARRY MURPHY

BASIC THROWN cylinders were transformed through modifications and additions into a wine decanter and cups.

DESIGN: MARILYN MAC KENZIE

FASCINATING animal shapes are expressed in outdoor planters. Because of size, planters were thrown in sections.

decoration...
form, texture, color

Watch a child as he feverishly covers a clean sheet of paper with crayon or paint; remember the pleasure of drawing patterns in the sand with your fingers or toes; or recall the anticipation of opening a fresh notebook, pen in hand, on the first day of school. Few of us can resist the challenge of a blank surface, including the potter when he begins to decorate clay.

Some clay shapes are strong enough to stand by themselves, without further ornamentation other than the natural color and texture of the clay. Generally, some type of decoration, whether it is worked into the surface of the clay or applied in the form of a stain or glaze, is necessary to complete the design. Remember that the decoration should complement and enhance a piece and be an integral part of the total design. Too often ornamentation is looked upon as a final step, and the result, not surprisingly, lacks the unity and harmony that comes from planning ahead. Keep in mind that a clay form can be embellished at any number of points in its development.

Decoration techniques in this chapter are arranged according to the effect they produce: altering the basic form of a piece, creating a dimensional surface texture, adding or changing the color. Examples of the methods discussed are illustrated within each section, but study all of the finished pieces shown throughout the book for inspiration and additional ideas.

The final four pages of this chapter are devoted to a portfolio of finished pieces, accompanied by descriptions of how each was decorated, to give you a better idea of how the various decorating techniques can be applied. As you study these pieces, you will notice that some methods, such as stamping, appear several times. Once you understand the individual techniques, you will be able to use each in numerous ways to create distinctive looking pieces.

In any creative endeavor, the final product mirrors the imagination and inventiveness of its maker. The tools don't make a handmade object unique; it's how the craftsman uses them to leave his personal mark on what he produces.

DESIGN: VIKTORIA CHULAY

COMBINATION of techniques — carving, oxides, and overall glaze — was used to decorate thrown, stoneware vase.

As you learn the specific techniques for decorating ceramic ware, you will see the possibilities and limitations of each method and be able to adapt them to your own needs. Don't be afraid to discuss techniques with other potters. Most will be happy to share with you their methods and ideas. Be as flexible as you can with decoration and use the information in this chapter as a starting point for your own explorations in form, texture, and color.

form

The shape of a still wet pot can be altered to improve its design or to achieve a particular decorative effect. How you manipulate the clay depends on the basic shape of the piece, and some shapes are best left quite simple. However, if you feel that the form will be enhanced by changing its contours, this can be accomplished with one of several tools or with your fingers.

Planes and angles can be developed by paddling the walls of your pot with a flat piece of wood or similar tool. Paddling will square off a rounded shape and round off, soften, or accentuate angular forms. This technique can be used to create pleasing asymmetry in an otherwise regular clay form.

Any flat object — a length of lumber, a butter paddle, or a piece of brick — will serve as a paddle. A tool with an irregular surface (the jagged edge of a broken board, a stick wrapped with rope and studded with tacks, or a board with a carved pattern) will create both texture and shape. Work with the paddle at different angles for special effects. The sharp edge of a flat stick will create definite ridges; either of the two wider sides will develop flat patches.

For paddling, clay shouldn't be too moist or the paddle will stick to it. If the clay is very stiff, cracks will result.

Pushing the walls of a pot in or out with your fingers or with a tool in a random or regular pattern can produce any number of exciting surfaces. If you push into the wall of a wet pot with the tip of your finger, you'll make a round indentation; a series of these concave impressions makes an attractive pattern. Pushing out from the inside with your fingertip will create an interesting bumpy surface.

A round jar or vase can be transformed into a multi-sided shape by using your finger to make evenly spaced vertical ridges along the inside walls of the pot. A corrugated surface can be created by working the ridges horizontally. Be careful not to press too hard against the clay or you might pierce the walls.

A pumpkin-like shape with a series of rounded projections is formed by fluting with either your fingers or a tool. If you use your fingers, the clay must be very flexible. Supporting the inside wall with one hand, run the index finger of the other hand vertically down the pot to form a ridge. Lobes develop when several ridges are spaced around the pot's circumference. If the ridges are close together, with only a thin strip of clay in between, the design resembles a carved Greek column.

A sharper impression is created by fluting a leather hard pot with a tool. You can fashion a fluting tool by carving one end of a flat stick into a point and the other end into a recessed semi-circle. The pointed end will create a groove when drawn along the clay. The curve will carve a double groove with a rounded projection between. A wire loop tool or a paper clip can also be used to make grooves.

DESIGN: ANDREE THOMPSON

DESIGN: JANE HORN

DESIGN: FRAN STEVENSON

FLUTING CREATED pumpkin-like effect on the body of a thrown teapot (left). Bowl (center) was paddled with edge of a flat stick to form texture. Round jar (right) became multi-sided when vertical ridges were made on its inside wall.

texture

Clay is an excellent medium for experiments in texture and pattern. At various stages, from wet to leather hard, clay will reproduce an impression, whether the mark be purposeful or the result of accidentally striking its surface with your hand or a tool.

Not every pot calls for a dimensional design. A stain, simple glaze, or even the natural clay may be all that is needed to complement a particular form. Texture, though, is always exciting and should be an integral part of a potter's decorating vocabulary.

When you are hand building or working on the wheel, impressions are sometimes made by fingers or by tools. These impressions don't have to be smoothed away; they can be left as decoration. Craftsmen have long realized that evidences of construction, such as joints and seams, can enhance the visual impact of their work.

You might want to think about surface embellishment in the early stages of making your piece, perhaps even before you take clay in hand. Patterns may develop as the result of the method used to form a piece, such as building with coils. Pre-texturing the clay (for example, on a coarsely woven cloth or over corrugated paper) will produce an overall pattern that would be difficult to achieve later on. Rolling a carved rolling pin, a hair curler, or a ball of twine (just three of an infinite number of objects around your house) over a slab will produce attractive designs.

When handling pre-textured clay, be careful not to erase or deform the pattern as you work. Texture can be restored along edges by re-pressing the blurred areas with whatever you used to make the initial impression. Be sure to align the fresh pattern with the original one.

Texturing with Found Objects

Clay will mimic whatever it comes in contact with. Since almost anything will make a design on the clay surface, look around for fresh ideas. A kitchen drawer offers forks, knives, paring tools, measuring spoons, potato mashers, pastry blenders, and pie crimpers. In the medicine cabinet, look at the tops of pill containers; they often have a ribbed edge which will produce a handsome pattern.

Inexpensive rubber stamps are obvious sources of texture (see spice jars, page 58), as are uncooked alphabet

spool of thread

lid from a tube

rubber bands

eucalyptus pod
fork
wire loop tool

edge of flat stick

lipstick tube
top of refillable pencil

thumb prints

SAMPLER of interesting textures made with "found" objects.

MARKS made in clay by your tools are sometimes attractive enough to be incorporated into the design of your piece.

CREATE overall texture on slab-built forms by rollings slabs out on nubby or coarsely woven fabric, such as burlap.

noodles glued to thin sticks (see cluster pots, page 28). A sewing box will yield buttons, spools of thread, safety pins, bobbins, and thimbles.

Actually, you needn't look any further than your fingers for a set of extremely versatile tools. Try dragging your finger tip along the clay or making regular incisions with the edge of your nail. Press into the clay with your knuckle or with the heel of your hand.

Natural objects such as bark, seed pods, pebbles, and leaves reproduce beautifully in clay. Texture need not be simply the result of a single or repeated impression of one object. Observe the delicate veins of a leaf or the swirling lines of grained wood and adapt the pattern to clay.

As you experiment with texturing objects, you'll learn the proper consistency of the clay for most effectively reproducing a particular pattern and at what point in the construction of your piece to apply texture. As a rule, softer lines and fuzzy edges occur when the clay is fairly wet, although if the clay is too moist, the tool may stick. Sharp impressions are made when the clay is leather hard.

Stamps for Impressions

Besides "found" objects, stamps are excellent tools for texturing. You can make your own by carving patterns into clay and then bisque firing them for durability. Or, you can carve stamps out of blocks of insulating brick, cork, styrofoam, plaster, or any other material that can be cut. Plaster may crumble if used frequently, so avoid plaster stamps for favorite patterns.

The library is a good source for design ideas. Look in pattern books for traditional motifs from foreign cultures around the world. Browse through yardage stores and study patterned cloth for inspiration, particularly the bold designs of Scandinavia, Africa, and Latin America.

If you see an especially pleasing texture, preserve it by pressing bits of clay into the pattern so that all the crevices are filled with clay. Carefully peel off the clay, add a handle, and let it dry. Then bisque-fire the clay.

Stamps can also be made from other stamps. You produce a negative of the original by making an impression on a slab of clay, cutting out the impression, adding a handle and then firing it. The new stamp will be slightly smaller than the original due to shrinkage of the clay.

If you have many stamps, it's often hard to remember what mark each will make. Make a visual reference file of your entire collection by impressing groups of stamps on slab tiles and firing the tiles.

How to make stamps. A stamp can be either a patterned cylinder that rolls along the surface of the clay to make a continuous impression, or a flat, patterned disc used for a single impression. For a rolling stamp, cut out a 1-inch-thick circle of clay with a biscuit cutter, pill box, or any sharp-edged cylinder of the desired diameter. With a smaller tube, cut a hole in the center of the disc. This hole will make it easier for you to roll the stamp across the clay. To make a flat stamp, pat out a lump of clay into a 1/2-inch-thick circle. Shape a knob and position it on one side of the

circle; attach by smearing the edges of the knob onto the circle. Let the stamps stiffen slightly before carving.

Adding decoration to stamps. To transfer a motif to the stamp, draw it first on paper with a felt tip marking pen. While the ink is still wet, place the drawing face down on the clay; then remove the paper. Go over the outline on the clay with a needle (this is necessary as the ink will probably fade before you are able to finish cutting out the design). Carve out the pattern with woodcarving or any clay carving tools that adapt to different designs. Patterns may also be carved freehand directly on the blank clay.

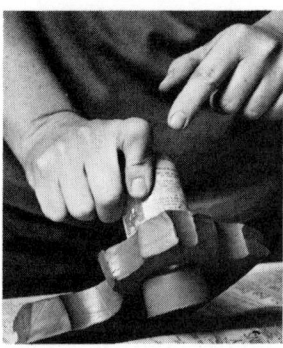 

USE 1-inch-thick circle of clay for a rolling stamp (left), 1/2-inch-thick clay disc with an attached knob for a flat stamp (right).

 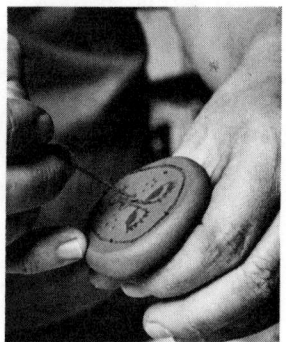

TO TRANSFER a pattern, press stamp onto inked drawing; trace outline into clay with needle before ink dries.

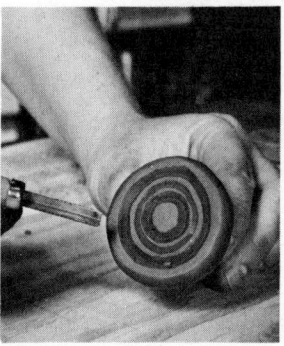 

CUT OUT patterns freehand, if you like. Woodcarving or linoleum block tools are good to use for carving.

Carving and Applied Decoration

Patterns can be created by partially or completely cutting into the clay wall. Any sharp tool makes a suitable carving device, but the particular tool you use will depend on the type of pattern you want. For crisp-edged designs, the clay must be stiff and not overly dry. Patterns cut into softer clay will have fuzzy edges.

Incised designs can be thin scratches or freeform curved or linear patterns made with a needle, fork or comb, or narrow wire or loop tool. For wider gouges, carve with a larger loop.

Raised or relief patterns, where the design projects from the background, are the result of cutting around the pattern.

If you are using a mold to shape your piece, carve a pattern into the mold surface so the clay will pick up the pattern. Cut patterns straight into the mold. Diagonal cuts may cause the clay in the mold to crack as it dries.

Piercing small openings in the walls of your pot or cutting out larger patterns is an effective technique when the design is highlighted from the inside with a candle. Enough clay must be left so the wall will stand firm. If the openings are small enough, they can be filled with a thin layer of translucent glaze. However, if they are too small, the glaze will plug up the holes and the "window" effect will be lost.

Clay in the form of buttons or thin coils can be added flat against the surface of your piece for raised textures. If applied to quite moist clay, buttons or coils don't need scoring or slip to adhere. However, it is safer to do both. Pressing or smearing the applied decoration with your finger or hatching across it with a needle will secure further the additions and at the same time create interesting patterns.

Entire motifs, geometric or freeform, can be cut out of a thin slab and "appliqued" to the pot, much like the applique patterns common in decorative stitchery. Scoring and slip replace needle, thread, or glue as the means to attach pattern to background.

Ornamental low relief motifs can be formed by pressing clay into a mold called a sprig mold, which has a pattern carved into it. English Wedgwood is famous for its sprigged decoration.

Bending or rolling coils into mazelike patterns and attaching them to a piece so that they stand away from the wall is another three-dimensional decorating technique. Fasten on the coil patterns as you would any attachment.

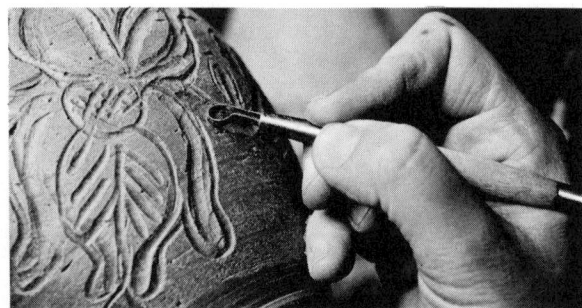

PATTERNS carved into leather-hard clay will be crisp and clean-edged. A ribbon tool is being used here to carve floral design.

DESIGN: HEIKO BOER

SERIES of graceful curls of clay were applied to give hanging planter delicate feeling (see also inside back cover).

DESIGN: LARRY MURPHY

CLAY BUTTONS were pressed to the wall of hanging planter and smeared with the thumb to make petaled "flower."

color

Color in any ceramic ware is the result of several factors: the color of the clay, the color applied to the clay, and the firing process.

Clay. Because iron is present in almost every clay, clay bodies fired to maturity will be generally warm in tone, ranging from a creamy buff to rich dark browns or even black (some clays will fire white). Both the temperature at which a clay is fired and the atmosphere in the kiln will affect the colors (see firing process, pages 74-77).

Clay color can be artificially changed through the use of metallic coloring oxides, such as iron oxide or manganese dioxide, or more simply by blending in commercially prepared body stains. The amount of oxides added must be carefully controlled, as some are strong fluxes which will lower the maturing temperature of the clay.

Adding grog of a contrasting color or oxides in granular form produce an attractive speckled effect. Inlaying a clay of a different color is still another way to achieve decorative color.

Applied color can be in the form of a slip or engobe, an oxide or stain, or a glaze, alone or in combination with an underglaze or an overglaze.

Slips and Engobes

A slip or engobe is a mixture of clay and water, often colored with oxides. Slips are used as decorative accents or to completely cover a clay body (both clay and slip must be of the same or of similar body composition) to provide a background for applied or incised decoration. Although the terms are used interchangeably, an engobe is often thought of as a slip that covers the surface of a pot.

Because clay is a major ingredient, slips can present shrinkage problems. Unless applied to very moist clay, slip decoration may crack or peel off as it dries or dissolve into the glaze applied over it. To counter these problems, slip mixtures often have additives that adjust shrinkage, alter the fusing temperature, increase opacity so that the color of the clay body will not show through, lighten the color, and promote a better glaze fit. The visual effect of a slip or engobe, whether clear bright color or muted, will depend on the type and composition of the glaze which covers it.

Apply slips and engobes on either raw or bisqued ware by brushing, sponging, dipping, pouring, spraying, stamping, or trailing with a special slip trailer, rubber syringe, or plastic squeeze bottle. For special decorative effects, use slips with the wax resist technique (see page 69) or mask an area with a stencil, apply slip, and remove the stencil when the slip is nearly dry. To slip transfer, dip textured materials, such as netting, string, or strips of paper, into colored slips, then press them into the raw clay surface. Peel the transfer materials off when the slip has almost dried or let it burn away during the bisque firing, leaving an impression of the original texture.

Mishima is the Japanese name for slip inlay. A piece is first decorated with impressed patterns, then covered with enough layers of slip of a different color than the clay so that the incised areas are filled. When dry, the slip is scraped away from the surface of the pot, leaving slip inlaid in the depressions.

Sgraffito is an Italian term for "scratched through." It involves applying slip over a leather-hard body; when the slip is almost dry, you scratch through one or more layers of slip with a pointed tool. This produces patterns from the contrast between slip and body color or between layers of different color slips.

DOTS, lines, circles, or freeform designs can be slip trailed with either a plastic squeeze bottle or a rubber syringe.

DESIGN: JEANNE SCHANZER
SGRAFFITO pattern was scratched through layer of dark-colored engobe to reveal lighter-colored clay body beneath.

Coloring Oxides and Stains

Metallic oxides and stains are used to give color to the clay body or to glazes. They can be used also under or over a glaze. Oxides commonly used as colorants are cobalt (oxide or carbonate), copper (oxide or carbonate), chrome oxide, iron oxide (red or black), manganese dioxide, nickel, rutile, and vanadium. Tin oxide and zirconium oxide make the glazes more opaque (opacifiers) and, if used without other colorants, whiter.

Beginners are advised to buy commercially prepared stains which are available in a wide range of colors, for making stains is a difficult process. Apply oxides or stains by brushing, sponging, or spraying.

To highlight texture, apply one or more thin coats of oxide over a bisqued piece until the impressions are filled. Wipe off the color from raised areas with a damp sponge.

Underglazes

Underglazes, used to decorate greenware or bisqued pieces, can be coloring oxides or pigments mixed with other ingredients to control color, insure adherence of the glaze to the body, permit ease of glaze application, and prevent the decoration from dissolving into the glaze. For permanence, a glaze is applied over an underglaze. A wide palette of reliable underglaze colors can be bought in pans like watercolors, in liquid form, or as crayons. Some colors are less stable and may dull or even disappear when fired at high temperatures.

Majolica

Majolica is a process whereby color is applied decoratively on an opaque, slightly damp, and glazed but unfired

MAJOLICA and metallic luster overglaze were used to decorate and tell a story on 16th century Italian plate.

surface (the base glaze is usually light in color or white). The glaze serves as a background for the decoration. Color is applied in the form of a colored glaze or underglaze that is brushed, trailed, or sprayed on. When fired, the surface colors fuse to the background glaze.

Majolica patterns can also be made by scratching through the glaze (use a glaze that will not close over the scratch marks during firing) to the clay body with a pin. After firing, the scratched lines show up as a linear design.

Overglazes

Overglazes (combinations of colorants, adherents, opacifiers, and a medium to promote ease of application) offer the greatest range of color for decorative purposes. These colors are applied to already glaze-fired pieces and fused by refiring at a lower temperature. Overglazes can be purchased.

Lusters are a thin coating of metal or iridescence deposited on the surface of a glaze and used as an overglaze. Color sets into the glaze through a low-temperature firing.

Glaze

A continuing source of pleasure and a time of great anticipation is the moment when the kiln is opened after a glaze firing. As ceramics is never predictable, exciting and surprising results can occur no matter how many times a particular glaze or decorating technique has been used.

The study of glazes and their formulation and application is a book in itself, and many fine volumes are available on this one topic alone. Following is a general overview of glazes and glazing to familiarize the beginner with this very important aspect of the craft.

A glaze is a glassy coating which fuses to the surface of the clay in the presence of heat. It is nonporous when fired to maturity, has great strength, imparts color or texture, and can protect underglaze decoration.

Basically, a glaze is composed of silica, a flux, and a refractory. Silica, the basic glass-forming material, would form a glaze alone, but to melt, silica needs temperatures out of the range of most kilns and beyond the melting point of clay. To lower the melting point of a glaze, a flux is needed. Fluxes, which also affect color and texture, vary in the temperature at which they liquify. Common fluxes are lead, sodium, lithium, potassium, barium, calcium, magnesium, zinc, and boron. To make a glaze less runny and to increase its strength and durability, a refractory, usually alumina in the form of clay, is added.

Other ingredients are introduced into the glaze to impart particular properties, such as opacity, matteness, brilliance of color, and correction of glaze faults. Metallic oxides are added for color.

Glazes are classified by appearance (glossy or matte, opaque, translucent or clear), color, temperature at which they should be fired, type of firing atmosphere (oxidation or reduction), and type of flux. Another factor is the presence of a frit (a pre-melted, cooled, and reground glass used as a glaze ingredient).

The following glazes are considered special because of their appearance, ingredients, or method of firing.

Ash. Fluid, semi-transparent glazes can be made by mixing the ashes of wood and vegetable matter with other glaze ingredients, such as feldspar and whiting. Ash glazes have been used for centuries, particularly by the Chinese and Japanese.

Crackle. Normally, fine lines or cracks in the surface of a glaze, called crazing, is considered a fault. Decorative crackles may be intentionally created by using a glaze that shrinks more than the clay body or by very rapid cooling of a glaze-fired piece. Raku ware often shows surface cracks because of the temperature extremes (see page 78). Cracks can be emphasized by rubbing over the surface of the glaze with ink or a coloring oxide, or if the piece is small enough, by boiling it in tea.

Crystalline glazing is a very special and carefully controlled procedure in which well-defined, individual crystals are grown in the glaze as it cools. This type of glaze is very runny in the kiln because of the very small amount or total absence of alumina. Aventurine glaze is a type of crystalline glaze where the entire glaze is made up of a crystalline structure, not always discernible as individual crystals.

Salt. Very popular in 19th century Europe and in this country, salt-glazed ware is easily recognizable by its characteristic pebbly "orange peel" texture. To salt glaze, salt (sodium chloride) is thrown into the kiln at the end of the firing cycle. As the salt vaporizes, the sodium combines with the silica in the clay body to form a glaze. At the same time, a toxic chlorine gas is released, so adequate ventilation around the kiln is essential. Although you can salt glaze bisqued ware, usually salt glazing is a one-fire process. Pieces are placed in the kiln unfired or green and are fired and glazed in a single step.

Buying glazes. Prepared glazes are available in liquid or powder form. Liquid glazes usually need only to be stirred to obtain the proper consistency. Occasionally they must be thinned with water, depending on how they will be applied. Powdered glazes are mixed with water (and sometimes with a gum for easier brushing) and strained to remove lumps. Many powders are base glazes to which oxides, stains, or other materials can be added. Powdered glazes are more economical than liquid ones.

Purchased glazes are grouped by color and texture (glossy or matte, clear, translucent or opaque) and the firing temperature. Sample glazed tiles are usually available

DESIGN: WILLIAM CREITZ

GREEN WOOD-ASH glaze with brushed and trailed pattern in white, blue, and brown slips decorates covered jar.

DESIGN: JACK FELTMAN

CRYSTALLINE glaze is shimmery pattern of individual crystals grown in glaze as it cools (see also inside back cover).

where you buy your glaze to give you an idea as to what the fired glaze will look like. Remember that its final appearance will depend on the color and texture of the clay underneath and the firing conditions to which the glaze will be subjected. Buy a glaze that fits the clay you are using and will fire in the temperature range of the kiln available to you.

Low-firing glazes generally melt from about cone 08 to cone 04 (1750° to 1950° F.). They tend to be soft, easily scratched, and somewhat water and acid soluble. High-firing glazes melt from cones 4 to 9 (2150° to 2350° F.) for stoneware and up to cone 14 (2500° F.) for porcelain. They tend to be very hard and insoluble in water and most acids. More brilliant colors are obtainable at low temperatures than at high temperatures.

Making glazes. Although you will find that buying glazes is easiest at first, you may want to make your own later on for economy and to expand the range of glazes available.

Glaze formulas are available in books and craft magazines and from other potters. Raw materials for glaze formulation are quite inexpensive and easily available from ceramic supply stores. You will also need cups or bowls for combining your ingredients, containers for storing glazes, measuring cups and spoons, a 60-mesh screen, a brush for applying the glaze, and an underglaze pencil (or a coloring oxide mixed with water and applied with a very thin brush) for marking test tiles.

Use bisqued tiles to test out glazes and save them for reference. Make tiles by throwing a very low cylinder, open at the bottom and with walls curving slightly upwards; slice into L-shaped wedges. The L-shaped wedges will demonstrate glaze performance on horizontal and vertical surfaces. You can also form tiles by slicing a thin slab into strips about 3 inches long and 1½ inches wide. Bend each strip to form an "L" and texture one area of the tile. If you punch a hole in each for stringing, you have a compact way to store the tiles.

Except for the simplest glaze recipes, dubbed "cup and spoon formulas" because of how they are measured, you will need a balance scale for very accurate ingredient measurement. Good balance scales are quite expensive, but if you are taking a ceramics class, most schools have them in the classroom.

To make a glaze, measure out the dry ingredients according to the formula, which will be expressed either in grams or percentages. Sprinkle the dry mixture over water and blend thoroughly. Use enough water in proportion to the dry ingredients so that the result is about the consistency of light cream. Pour the glaze through a screen to remove lumps. Transfer the glaze to a labeled container.

The glaze is now ready to use. It's a good idea to test the glaze on bisqued tiles before using on a finished piece. Mark the tiles with the underglaze pencil or with an oxide to indicate the glaze composition.

Only by experimentation will you gain an understanding of the interrelationship of glaze materials, the particular effects of each ingredient, and how to adjust glaze formulas to fit a clay body.

Applying glaze. Glaze is usually applied to pots that have been bisque fired. Glazing raw, or unfired, clay is possible but risky because the pieces are fragile and their capacity to absorb moisture may cause cracks.

Prepare bisqued ware for glazing by sponging off all dust and dirt or by holding under running water. (Do not overwet or soak the piece.) The water will reduce the porosity of the clay so that it will accept the correct amount of glaze.

The thickness of the glaze mixture depends on how porous the pot. A less porous piece requires a thicker glaze; a more open pot needs a thinner glaze. The amount of glaze applied should be no more than 1/16 of an inch.

To prevent the glaze from sticking to the kiln shelf, coat the bottom and ¼ inch up the sides of the pot with melted wax. Wipe off beads of glaze that remain on the wax.

If you glaze fire a container with a lid in place, remember not to glaze areas that will touch.

Glaze can be applied in several ways. *Brushing* is good

TO ACCURATELY measure your raw materials when preparing glazes from a formula, you need a balance scale.

BRUSH WAX on bottom and lower walls of your pot; it repels glaze that may cause the pot to stick to the kiln shelf.

for small pieces. Brush-glazing large pots is time consuming, and, since only a small area can be covered at one time, this technique may result in an uneven glaze coat. Use a flat brush and apply several layers of glaze to get the proper thickness.

Pouring is used to coat the insides of a pot, particularly narrow-necked shapes that cannot be reached any other way. Pour glaze, of a thinner consistency than for brushing or dipping, into the interior of the piece, quickly rotate the piece to spread the glaze evenly, and spill out excess liquid. Repeat the process to cover the walls completely.

To glaze the outside walls, hold the piece over a pan to catch the extra glaze or rest the pot on sticks or on a rack set across the pan; then pour on the glaze.

Dipping requires the largest amount of glaze, but it is probably the easiest to do. Coat the insides of the pot first by pouring. Holding the pot by its foot or near its rim with your fingers or with tongs, immerse into the glaze. Pull it out almost immediately and shake to remove excess glaze. Touch up bare spots from fingers or tongs with a brush. Partial dipping in several colors of glaze produces an attractive finish, particularly where glazes overlap.

Spraying, accomplished with a spray gun or atomizer, requires a special booth set up around the pot to catch extra glaze and must be done in a well-ventilated area. Spraying results in an even application of the glaze.

Other decorative techniques can be used in connection with engobes and glazes. *Wax resist* is a process whereby wax is brushed on a pot in areas where you want the body color exposed. When glaze is applied over the piece, it will bead off the wax, which melts away in the kiln. Wax can also be applied over a coat of glaze which is then given another glaze coating. The first glaze will show up in a pattern after the wax melts. Or, designs can be scratched through a wax coat. The piece is then dipped into a colorant or glaze which will penetrate only the incised areas. Use either liquid wax or paraffin.

The *sgraffito* technique (see page 65) is effective with glazes as well as with slip. Patterns can be made by scratching through the still damp glaze to an undercolor or the clay body itself.

Glazes can also be *trailed* like slips or *squirted* on, using a rubber syringe.

POUR ON glazes to coat the interior of pots, especially narrow-necked ones, that are difficult to reach with other methods.

SPRAYING ON a glaze gives an even coating, although it requires a special, ventilated booth and a spray gun.

DIPPING requires more glaze than brushing or pouring. Try partially dipping a pot in several different glazes.

TO WAX RESIST, brush on designs with wax. Wax repels the glaze, leaving a pattern after it melts in the kiln.

potpourri of decorating techniques

On this and the following three pages is an assemblage of ceramic pieces that illustrate numerous decorating techniques available to the potter. Note the versatility of each method. Imaginative designs can be simple (incising) or complex (trailing slips). Always be adventurous and experiment with your decorative touches.

DESIGN: GLENN SPANGLER

STRIPES OF STAIN, applied over a sprayed-on white glaze, bled when vase was fired (see also inside back cover).

DESIGN: ELIZABETH HEIL

SLIP-TRAILED DOTS emphasize round contours of thrown stoneware pitcher. Inside, neck, and handle are glazed.

DESIGN: BONNIE IKEMURA

MULTI-COLOR OXIDE and slip design under translucent glaze decorate stoneware mugs (see also inside front cover).

DESIGN: WALTRAUD WEBER

DELICATE sgraffito design was produced by cutting through a tan glaze to an undercoat of dark-colored slip.

INTRIGUING "profile" handle of thrown porcelain cup was cut from a thin slab of clay and then attached to the cup.

DESIGN: ANDREE THOMPSON

DESIGN: GREGOR GIESMANN

A SPECIAL PROCESS that involves transferring a photographic image via decal to pot was used for this jar.

DESIGN: E. D. TAYLOR

LETTERING on hand-built "News Pot" was pressed into leather-hard clay with plaster impression of newspaper mat.

DESIGN: BOB NICHOLS

LAYER of white glaze was partially scratched away to reveal darker glaze beneath, creating swirling dot pattern.

DESIGN: WALTRAUD WEBER

OVERLAPPING LAYERS of poured white glaze over an iron oxide wash create shadowy effects on stoneware pot.

DESIGN: DIANA LEON

COBALT OXIDE applied with a sponge onto a coat of dried, white glaze resulted in mottled pattern on porcelain jar.

DESIGN: TONI WILLIAMSON

STAMPS were pressed into walls of hand-built, stained bowl and also into bits of clay attached to its surface.

DESIGN: SANDRA JOHNSTONE

SALT-GLAZED container's strong design stems from bold use of applied clay decoration, engobes, and oxides.

DESIGN: VERONICA DOLAN

SLAB BOTTLE was rolled out on burlap, curved into cylindrical shape, decorated with tool marks, and left unglazed.

DESIGN: RICH KITSON

INCISED RINGS, formed while piece was on wheel, texture lid and handle of casserole (also see inside back cover).

DESIGN: ELIZABETH HEIL

STONEWARE JUG has glazed neck, shoulder, handle; bare bottom; brightly glazed stamped medallion (see also front cover).

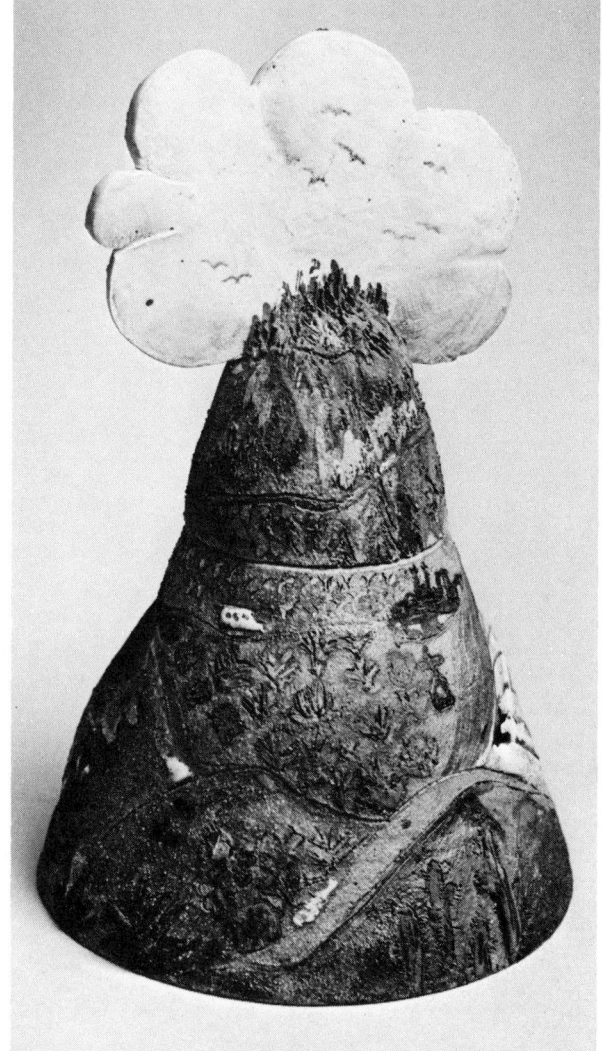

DESIGN: ANDREE THOMPSON

"MOUNTAIN JAR" of stoneware and porcelain charmingly depicts a trip to Mexico. Piece is thrown, except for cloud.

DESIGN: TONI WILLIAMSON

BOLD DAISY pattern was created on hand-built piece by brushing wax on bisqued clay, then dipping it in white glaze.

firing...
its effect and equipment

The transformation of clay from a fragile form (which will disintegrate if soaked in water) into a hard, fused material (impervious to moisture) involves a complex series of physical and chemical changes accomplished by subjecting the raw ware to heat. This firing process takes place in a kiln where clay is exposed to controlled heat for a length of time until the desired effect has been reached. The firing is followed by a gradual cooling cycle that lasts at least as long as the firing.

The cooling period is very important. If the kiln is opened prematurely, before the pieces have been allowed to cool sufficiently to withstand the shock of sudden exposure to the relatively low room and atmospheric temperatures, the ware will probably crack or sections of the glaze will peel off. It's best to wait until the temperature of the kiln has dropped to below 300° F. or until the pieces can be removed with bare hands.

Ware is subjected generally to two firings. The first (or bisque) firing is most often accomplished at about 1800° F. (cone 07 to 06). This firing allows the clay to develop enough strength to be handled safely, yet still be porous enough to accept glaze. Bisque firings are slow — from 6 to 12 hours, depending on the size and thickness of the pieces, the size of the kiln, and the kiln load.

In the second (or glaze) firing, glazed or otherwise decorated bisqued ware is fired to the maturing temperature of clay and glaze. There are exceptions, such as raku (see page 78), where a low-fire glaze is used over a high-fire clay body and fired to the fusing temperature of the glaze only. Fusing overglazes on pieces which have already gone through two firings requires a lower temperature firing than the original maturing temperature of the clay and background glaze. As a rule, however, a glaze is selected that will reach maturity at the same point as the clay.

Effect of heat on clay. Although a clay object might appear completely dry when put into the kiln for the bisque firing, it still contains moisture that must be removed. To complete the drying, the loaded kiln is set at a low temperature for about $1/2$ hour to an hour, with the door ajar to allow moisture and gases to escape. Often a full kiln will be left on

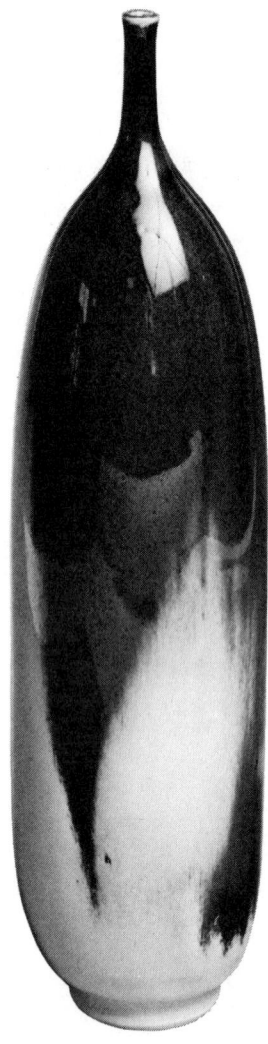

REDUCTION FIRING produced copper red streaks in glaze on this porcelain bottle (also see inside back cover).

low overnight (if it is fuel burning, with just the pilot light on) for the initial drying and then turned up in the morning.

As the temperature increases, chemically combined water present in the clay is driven off, organic materials burn away, and the clay reaches the point of dehydration. Changes occur in crystal structure, along with fluctuations in volume. Finally, the clay hardens or vitrifies, and, at the same time, undergoes further shrinkage. The vitrification point varies with the clay body composition, although any clay heated beyond its maturing temperature will eventually slump and become molten.

Kilns

All kilns are made up of heat-resistant materials which will withstand the high temperatures to which clay is fired, confine and concentrate heat to the firing chamber, and allow for a gradual heat loss during cooling. Added to the basic structure is a method of introducing heat, such as gas burners or metal alloy elements of an electric kiln, into the chamber.

Although specific kiln designs vary, they are generally typed in three ways: 1) by whether they are electric or fuel burning (also the type of fuel used); 2) by the temperature range they can achieve (low-fire kilns fire up to about cone 8, approximately 2300° F., high-firing kilns can reach cone 14, about 2500° F.); and 3) by their size.

Kilns can be purchased, although many potters prefer to build their own to save money or to get a kiln of a particular design. Plans for building kilns are available from books, craft magazines, and stores. Materials can be purchased from ceramic dealers, building and brick suppliers, and sheet metal suppliers.

Electric kilns are easy to operate, safe, clean firing, and run on household current. They are relatively portable (many come on casters) and can be transported. As heat is evenly distributed, electric kilns are fairly predictable. A low-fire elecric kiln with interior dimensions of approximately 11 x 11 x 13 inches will cost approximately $100.

Electric kilns always fire in oxidation, and many glazes and decorative effects are geared to an oxidizing atmosphere. A major disadvantage of electric kilns is that a reduction atmosphere is difficult to obtain without badly damaging the elements. Then, too, ware fired in an electric kiln may lack the richness of color and surface interest of pieces fired in reduction, though most low-fire glazes do give a lustrous and glossy appearance.

An electric kiln has another disadvantage. While the kiln itself will last indefinitely, the kiln elements will have to be replaced.

Fuel-burning kilns require a chimney and, although they can be dismantled, are generally considered permanent installations. Heat is not as evenly distributed in fuel-burning kilns as in electric ones. However, the great attraction of fuel-burning kilns is that both oxidation and reduction can be achieved in the same unit.

An oxidizing atmosphere is one in which an ample supply of oxygen is present to combine with carbon to form carbon dioxide. If this oxygen supply is reduced, the carbon will turn to the oxygen in the metallic oxides in the clay and the glaze and will effect a change in their color, usually making the clay warmer and earthier in appearance and the glazes richer and more varied in texture. Any free carbon may settle in the ware, changing the clay color to shades of grey or black (as in raku).

In a reduction atmosphere, special reduction glazes will change color completely — iron in low percentages changes to grey-greens, in higher concentrations to dark rust browns or black; copper changes to shades of red and pink. Reduction firings begin and end in oxidation. Generally, reduction is done heavily at about cone 8 for about ½ hour and gradually brought up to a moderate reduction for the remainder of the firing cycle. Oxidation takes place for the last 5 minutes or so to clear the kiln.

Kiln Furniture

The kiln interior may be divided with refractory shelves and posts for the most efficient use of space. Shelves come in a variety of shapes, sizes, and thicknesses and vary in price, depending on their dimensions and composition.

Special square or triangular posts are also available in a range of sizes to allow for flexibility in loading pieces of different sizes. Hard brick is also used as shelf supports and can be cut to size.

The top surface of all shelves are usually given several coats of kiln wash to prevent runny glazes from fusing a pot to the shelf. Kiln wash (a mixture of equal parts of flint and kaolin, plus water and the consistency of heavy cream) can be purchased or made up. If pots or blobs of glaze stick to the shelf, they can be peeled off, along with the kiln wash. Bare patches, where the kiln wash was removed, must be touched up. When the kiln wash has become too uneven from patching, it must be removed (use a silicon carbide grinder), and new coats applied. Kiln wash should not be applied to the very edge of the shelf. Leave about a ½-inch margin, for the kiln wash can chip off and fall into and damage ware on a lower shelf.

If a piece must be glazed completely, set it on a stilt or prop of some sort so it won't stick to the shelf. Marks made on the ware by the stilts are usually unobtrusive. Firebrick and insulating brick may also be used for propping ware. If vertical space is a problem, brick can be crumbled and the crumbs arranged into a low bed to support a pot with a runny glaze.

String glazed beads and jewelry on special nichrome wire to prevent sticking.

FIREBRICK and refractory shelves (heat resistant) and posts divide interior space of kiln and support ware during firing.

Loading the Kiln

Ware is loaded into the kiln differently for the bisque and glaze firings. With both firings, though, the most even distribution of heat will result from a uniformly loaded kiln.

Raw ware can be stacked for bisquing, since bisqued pieces will not stick together as they cool. Smaller pieces can be placed inside larger ones — don't set heavier pieces over weaker ones and avoid stresses.

Glazed pieces must not touch, for if they do, the glazes will fuse the pieces together during cooling. Leave 1/8 to 1/4 inch between unfired glazed pieces in the kiln. The bottoms and 1/4 inch up the sides should be either dry-footed or wiped free of glaze.

In both firings, leave up to 1/2 inch between ware and the kiln walls.

Temperature Measurement

Time and temperature play an important role in the firing process. Knowing the interior temperature of the kiln is helpful (a *pyrometer* is often used), but temperature by itself is not a sufficient indicator of the progress of the pieces being fired. A particular temperature may be reached by a rapid increase in heat, but the clay may not have had the time to undergo the necessary changes.

Many factors influence the kiln temperature, including how close to capacity the kiln has been loaded and the distribution of the pieces within the kiln. A closely packed area of a kiln will differ in temperature from another area which has fewer or smaller pieces. A smaller kiln will heat up faster than a larger one; a less-than-full kiln will heat up faster than one fully loaded.

The prime concern in firing clay and glazes is knowing when the pieces being fired have reached the desired state. Very experienced potters can judge temperature by the color of the kiln interior. With increasing temperature, heat changes in color from dull red to a brighter red, orange, yellow, and finally bright white. However, most potters rely on pyrometric cones as a measure of the combined effects of time and temperature.

Pyrometric cones are thin pyramids of ceramic material that will deform or bend at a particular time-temperature condition. They are not used as a measure of temperature but rather as a measure of the work done by heat on the pieces being fired.

Cones can be purchased in two sizes: large cones are 2 1/2 inches high, with a 1/2-inch base; small cones are 1 1/8

FOR A BISQUE FIRING, ware is stacked in kiln, since bare clay pieces will not stick together in this first firing.

FOR A GLAZE FIRING, space is left between pieces to prevent sticking. Load was just fired — note cones.

inches high and have a ¼-inch base. Generally, larger cones are preferred because they are easier to see. Small cones are used where space is limited or in connection with an automatic shut-off device. Because of its size, the large cone will bend about 25° sooner than the small cone, although this difference is usually unimportant.

Cones are referred to by number. These numbers match an approximate temperature that varies, depending upon the rate of temperature rise per hour. The lowest cone is numbered 022. As the numbers decrease (021, 020, 019, up to 01), an increase in heat is indicated. After 01, the 0 is dropped and the numbers progress upwards to 42, which is the highest. Most potters work within the range of cone 020 to about cone 12.

Usually, cones are used in series of three. For example, if you are firing to cone 9, you would use cones 8, 9, and 10. The cones are so arranged that when the lowest numbered cone bends, it will soon be time to end the firing cycle. When the middle cone deforms, the ware is ready. Bending of the highest numbered cone means that the pieces are probably overfired.

Cones can be set in special, porous cone plaques or in individual metal holders. Make your own plaque by setting three cones, each at an angle (at 8°), so the base rests flat in a lump of clay of the same composition as the ware being fired and punching holes in the clay to prevent explosions. Make sure the plaques are completely dry before they are used.

Place cones on the kiln shelf so they are visible through the peep holes. In larger kilns, temperature may differ from top to bottom and from back to front, so you may want to place cones at various spots around the kiln.

Where to Fire

If you don't have your own kiln and aren't currently enrolled in a ceramics class or workshop, consult ceramic supply stores, schools, recreation centers, and local potters. Usually your work will be fired for a fee based on the size of your piece. It's wise to locate a kiln source before making a piece. This way you can choose clays and glazes that will fire to the temperature of that particular kiln.

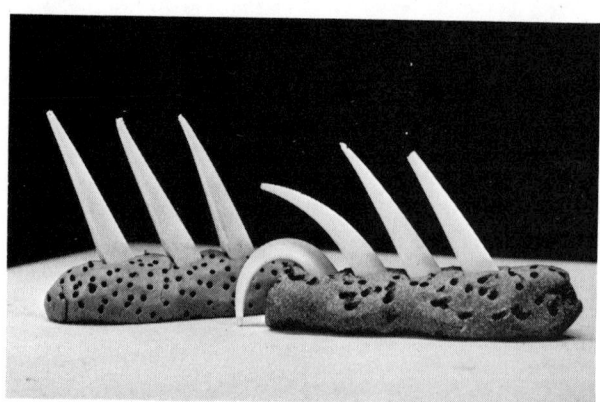

PYROMETRIC CONES, used in threes or fours, measure heat in kiln. At left are unfired cones; at right, fired cones.

TEMPERATURE EQUIVALENTS FOR ORTON STANDARD PYROMETRIC CONES

CONE NUMBER	TEMPERATURE EQUIVALENT*	CONE NUMBER	TEMPERATURE EQUIVALENT*
021	1137°F.	03	2014°F.
020	1175	02	2048
019	1261	01	2079
018	1323	1	2109
017	1377	2	2124
016	1458	3	2134
015	1479	4	2167
014	1540	5	2185
013	1566	6	2232
012	1623	7	2264
011	1641	8	2305
010	1641	9	2336
09	1693	10	2381
08	1751	11	2399
07	1803	12	2419
06	1830	13	2455
05	1915	14	2491
04	1940	15	2608

*When temperature increased 270°F. per hour, large cones. Courtesy the Edward Orton Jr. Ceramic Foundation.

raku...
special firing method

Raku, meaning "enjoyment" or "pleasure," is a procedure for making pottery that was developed in Japan toward the end of the 16th century. Simple raku pots and bowls were created primarily for use in Zen tea ceremonies.

Although the raku-firing technique was introduced in this country in the early 1900s, only recently have American potters experimented with the process and has it achieved wide popularity.

Raku, as practiced in this country, involves a very rapid firing of pieces (unglazed or coated with low-fire glazes), which are then removed hot from the kiln and placed in leaves or other combustible material for reduction. The material and the pots are placed in a container as airtight as possible for this reduction. Glazed raku pieces may have a luster and frequently a crackle. Unglazed surfaces turn a rich black or smoky grey.

Because of their spontaneity and unpredictable results, raku firings are exciting to watch or participate in. The entire process takes about one hour, compared to 12 to 24 hours for a stoneware firing. Since the process is so fast, you can watch the glaze go from a dry powder to a boiling mass and then to a melted, glassy, fused finish.

DESIGN: DANIEL OBERTI

RAKU BOTTLE, with copper engobe over porcelain slip, has extruded slip decoration (see also inside front cover).

When planning a piece to be raku-fired, several factors should be kept in mind. Since the clay must withstand rapid changes in temperature, use a high-firing stoneware clay containing a good deal of grog (even 30 percent) or sand.

When deciding what to make, remember that a raku firing takes place at a relatively low temperature (1700° to 1900° F. range). Therefore, raku pieces are rather soft, having the strength of earthenware, not of stoneware, and may not be waterproof.

STANFORD UNIVERSITY MUSEUM OF ART   DESIGN: VERONICA DOLAN   DESIGN: PAUL SOLDNER; PRIETO COLLECTION, MILLS COLLEGE

EXAMPLES of raku are 16th century Japanese tea bowl (left), contemporary American pieces (center and right). Thrown bowl (center) uses glaze, oxide; hand-built pot (right; see also inside front cover) uses slip, oxides, glaze.

Pots should be made from one piece of clay or with as few joints or additions as possible because of the severe and sudden heat changes. When constructing pieces, make walls an even ¼ to ½-inch thick. Pieces that are too thick or too thin or of uneven thickness are subject to cracking or warping.

Bisque fire your piece first. The raku firing is too rapid for the clay to have enough time to undergo the complex chemical and physical changes that transform it from mud to ceramic without shattering.

Glazes. You can buy glazes for raku (use a low-fire glaze — cone 08 to 04), or you can mix your own. For a clear glaze, combine equal parts of borax and colemanite and enough water to make a creamy mixture. To make colored glazes, add ½ to 1 teaspoons of coloring oxide to each ½-cup glaze. Iron oxide gives brown, black, or brick red tones; copper oxide or carbonate give a turquoise color (if unreduced) or metallic copper look (if reduced); cobalt oxide or carbonate make for brilliant blues; rutile will produce a mustard yellow. Bright red, yellow, and orange are generally obtained through lead base glazes; these should *not* be used on the inside of food or beverage containers.

Brush, dip, or pour a glaze onto the bisqued piece. Areas covered with transparent glaze will remain the color of the clay body or oxide; unglazed parts will be black, or where oxides are left bare, very subtle in color. Let the glaze dry (usually one-half to one hour) before raku firing. Glazed pieces are customarily preheated on top of the kiln before being placed in it. Preheating takes place while another load is being fired. You may want to glaze a day ahead, for if the glaze drying is hurried, the expansion of steam may cause the pieces to crack or break.

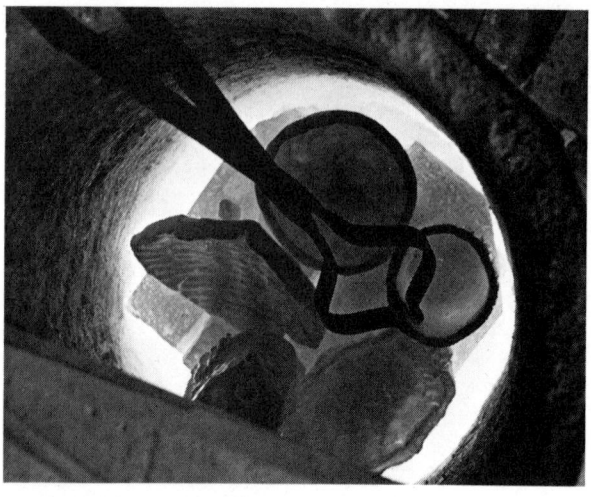

1) IN A RAKU FIRING, remove the hot pieces from the kiln with tongs when glaze has a shiny, wet appearance.

2) TO REDUCE the red-hot ware, after removing from kiln place immediately in combustible materials in an air-tight container.

3) DIP FIRED PIECES in water for rapid cooling. If pots are poorly constructed, sudden heat change may cause cracking.

4) IN COLLECTION of raku-fired ware, note smoky black areas; this is where the unglazed clay was reduced.

glossary

Ash glaze: Semi-transparent glaze containing ashes of wood or vegetable matter.

Ball clays: High-firing, natural, fine-grained, plastic; high shrinkage rate.

Banding wheel: Round turntable used in hand building and in applying glazes.

Bat: Portable work surface, usually round, made of plaster, wood, or plastic-topped composition board, for use in hand building or on the wheel.

Bisque: The state of ware after its first firing, to about 1800°F. (cone 07-06).

Centering: Adjusting clay so it rests in exact center of wheel head for throwing.

Chuck: Usually a bisqued clay cylinder, temporarily attached to wheel for trimming narrow-necked pieces.

Crackle glaze: Intentionally fostered fine lines or cracks in the surface of a glaze.

Crystalline glaze: Well-defined individual crystals grown in glaze's surface as it cools.

Earthenware: Single, natural clay or mixture of several clays, relatively low-firing; remains porous when fired.

Engobe: Slip generally used to change color of clay surface.

Fireclays: Extremely high-firing clay used to make firebrick, to line kilns, for kiln shelves and posts.

Flux: Material added to glaze (or occurring in clay) that lowers firing temperature and affects glaze color and appearance.

Frit: Pre-melted, cooled, reground glass used as glaze ingredient to render materials insoluble.

Glaze: Glassy coating which fuses to surface of clay in the presence of heat.

Greenware: Raw, dried, and unfired ware.

Grog: Finely ground, fired clay added to clay body to reduce shrinkage and plasticity or to impart texture.

Kaolin: Pure, natural clay, white, relatively lacking in plasticity, highly heat-resistant.

Kiln: Heat-resistant device used to fire ceramic ware.

Leather hard: State reached by clay during drying when it can be textured and pieces joined without danger of deforming.

Luster: Overglaze decoration; thin coating of metal or iridescence placed on surface of glaze and set into glaze through low-temperature firing.

Majolica: Decorative technique; color is applied to opaque, slightly damp, unfired glazed surface or patterns are scratched through this glaze.

Maturing temperature: When clay or glaze achieves desired characteristics.

Mishima: Decorative technique; slip applied over textured clay is scraped away from surface when dry, leaving slip in depressions.

Overglaze: Decorative technique; color applied to already glazed and fired piece is fused through low-temperature firing; also a colorant.

Oxidation: Firing method in which ample supply of oxygen is present in kiln.

Paddling: Beating clay with flat stick to strengthen joints, thin walls, alter shape, create texture.

Plasticity: Ability of clay to deform under pressure and retain new shape without cracking.

Porcelain: Compounded clay, very high firing, white, translucent, very hard and vitreous when fired.

Pyrometer: Device to indicate internal temperature of kiln during firing.

Pyrometric cones: Thin pyramids of ceramic material; measure heat in kiln during firing.

Raku: Japanese firing process. In this country, it involves the rapid firing of ware, removed hot from kiln and reduced by covering with combustible material.

Reduction: Firing with reduced oxygen supply in kiln.

Reduction glaze: Develops its characteristics only in reduction atmosphere.

Refractory: High resistance to heat.

Salt glaze: Salt vaporizes in kiln, coating ware and leaving pebbly, "orange-peel" texture.

Sgraffito: Decorative technique; design is scratched through one or more layers of slip or glaze, producing patterns from contrast between layers or between slip and clay.

Slip: Suspension of clay in water; used as "glue" or for decoration.

Stain: Single coloring oxide or oxides in combination with other materials used as a colorant or as decoration.

Stoneware: High-firing clays, hard and vitrified when fired; color ranges from light tans to darker greys.

Throwing: Making ware on potter's wheel.

Vitreous: Like glass.

Wax resist: Decorative technique; wax is applied to raw, bisqued, or glazed ware to repel overcoat of slip or glaze.

---

index